MW01041798

HISTORICAL
MARKERS
OF WILLIAMSON
COUNTY
TENNESSEE

About This Book

This book is divided into seven parts, each consisting of a specific city, community, or area. Following the parts as they appear takes the reader through an almost clockwise trip across the county, beginning in Brentwood and ending in Franklin. Maps are provided at the beginning of each part to guide travelers, and the exact text of each marker, along with a description of its location, is given. The following symbols are used throughout the book to designate those who have placed markers in Williamson County.

 Brentwood Historical Commission

 Tennessee Historical Commission/ Society

 Daughters of the American Revolution

 United Daughters of the Confederacy

 Heritage Foundation of Franklin/ Williamson County

 Williamson County Historical Society

HISTORICAL MARKERS
OF WILLIAMSON
COUNTY
TENNESSEE

A Pictorial Guide

Rick Warwick

HILLSBORO PRESS
Franklin, Tennessee

TENNESSEE HERITAGE LIBRARY
Bicentennial Collection

Copyright 1999 by Rick Warwick

All rights reserved. Written permission must be secured from the publisher to use or reproduce any part of this book, except for brief quotations in critical reviews or articles.

Printed in the United States of America

03   02   01   00   99   1   2   3   4   5

Library of Congress Catalog Card Number: 99-65240

ISBN: 1-57736-147-4

Cover design by Gary Bozeman

Location maps by Cliff Eanes-Tierney

Published by
HILLSBORO PRESS
An imprint of
PROVIDENCE HOUSE PUBLISHERS
238 Seaboard Lane • Franklin, Tennessee 37067
800-321-5692
www.providencehouse.com

To local historians

Virginia McDaniel Bowman	Susie Gentry	Park Marshall
Colonel Campbell Brown	Colonel John L. Jordan	Marshall Morgan
Dr. Rosalie Carter	T. Vance Little	Jane Bowman Owen
John Weakley Covington	Louise Gillespie Lynch	Dan Robison
Judge W. W. Faw	Lula Fain Major	William S. Webb

whose legacy has enriched our understanding of the past.

Without their research,

scholarship, and interest in

Williamson County,

our heritage would be poorer

and our history largely unrecorded.

CONTENTS

PREFACE AND ACKNOWLEDGMENTS

 For the past decade or so the Williamson County Historical Society has overseen the placement of historic markers throughout the county. In 1991 Society President Robert Hicks appointed Ridley Wills II to chair a marker committee along with County Historian Virginia Bowman and Society members Jane Trabue, Jack Gaultney, and Vance Little. In 1995 County Executive Robert Ring approached Commissioner Judy Hayes and myself about co-chairing a Tennessee Bicentennial Committee to manage projects and programs in Williamson County for a two-year period. Judy and I were fortunate to assemble a group of hardworking, enthusiastic committee members consisting of Nancy Bassett, Thelma Battle, Nancy Conway, Leo Goodsell, Jay Johnson, Janice Keck, Ann Lynch, Linda Lynch, Margaret McGehee, E. J. Neeley, Sue Oden, Judy Parnell, Mary Pearce, Cletus Sickler, Betty Stewart, Tom Stillwell, Diane Sylvis, Tracie Thurmond, Tony Turnbow, and Linda Woodside.

Recognizing the benefits of marking historic sites for tourists, newcomers, and natives of the county, the Bicentennial Committee selected the placement of markers as a primary project. When necessary, seed money was offered communities to help raise the thirteen hundred and twenty-five dollars to cover the cost of a marker. Remarkably, under the Bicentennial project, sixty-two markers popped up across the county. Considering the earlier efforts of the Williamson County Historical Society, the Brentwood Historical Commission, and the Heritage Foundation, the total number of new markers since 1991 approaches ninety. As the success of this program suggests, Williamson County is historic and proud of it.

The publishing of a handbook of marker texts and period photographs was the brainchild of Brentwood historian Vance Little. Jack and Tina Gaultney

9

were responsible for photographing the twenty-five state highway markers, many placed in the 1960s and 1970s in inconvenient locations along heavily traveled roadways. Also, the Gaultneys sought out the Brentwood Historical Commission markers and other tablets, plaques, and markers located in Franklin and rural Williamson County. Mary Pearce and I approached Allan Patton of the Fieldstone development, who had expressed interest in helping the Heritage Foundation, to underwrite the production of this book. We then met with the president of the Williamson County Historical Society, Andrew B. Miller, about a publishing contract, and the rest is, as they say, history.

Personally, I have received great satisfaction in working with the many communities, committees, and individuals who shared my interest in preserving the heritage of this county. With a quick glance at a county map locating historic markers, I am satisfied few districts have been overlooked. Special thanks are due Sadye Tune Wilson, Nancy Fitzgerald, Beverly Overbey, Camille Allen, Gail Gilley, Sara Rodes Lee, Walter Lee Jordan, Ennis Wallace, Aubrey Preston, Joey Davis, Glenn Casada, David Ogilvie, and Frank Wilson for their financial and informational support in placing markers in their communities. Also, thanks to County Highway Superintendent Charles Meeks and Franklin Street Supervisor Wilson Vaden for erecting markers. Over 150 thousand dollars has been raised for historic markers in the last decade, largely from small donations of interested citizens.

Grateful appreciation to Andrew B. Miller and the dedicated staff at Providence House Publishers. Special thanks to Elaine Kernea Wilson for layout and design, Debbie Sims and Marilyn Friedlander for editing and proofreading, and Holly Jones for supervision of production/editorial. Because of their combined publishing expertise, *Historical Markers of Williamson County* is a useful and beautiful Hillsboro Press addition to the *Tennessee Heritage Library* from Providence House Publishers.

Photography and illustration credits are due to the following artisans: Dr. Rosalie Carter, 147, 173; Chappel, 92; Susie Gentry, 172; Bob Holladay, 22, 58, 59, 71, 108; Henry Inman, 131; J. B. Longacre, 131; Annie Owen, 132; Sanborn-Perris Map Co., 133, 158; L. T. Shull, 174; Bill Vantrease, 39; Rick Warwick, 20, 37, 69, 70, 72, 73, 93, 98, 110, 159, 161, 162; William S. Webb, 48.

On October 26, 1999, Williamson County will celebrate its 200th birthday. May this publication prove useful in making our history more readily available. May future generations appreciate our efforts and safeguard their legacy.

RESOURCES

The author is appreciative of the assistance he received in gathering illustrations reproduced in this book. The following is a listing of the contributors of those illustrations and the pages on which they appear.

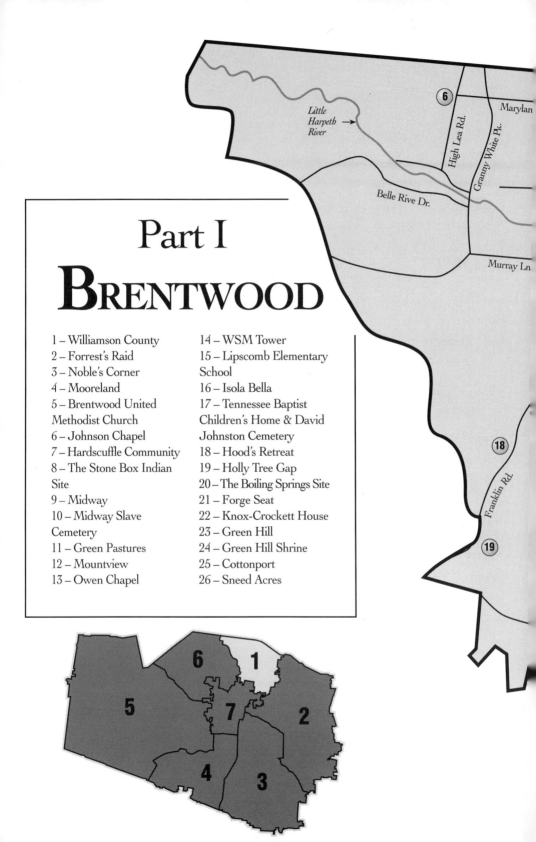

Part I

BRENTWOOD

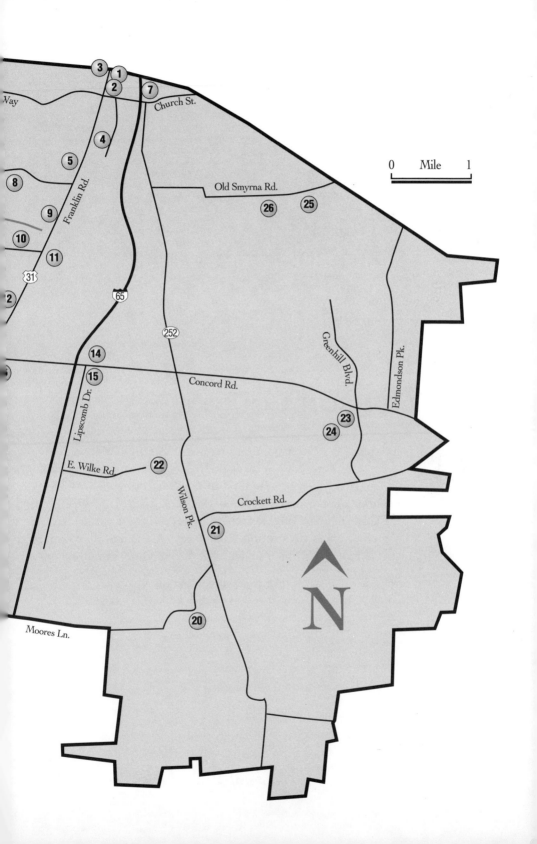

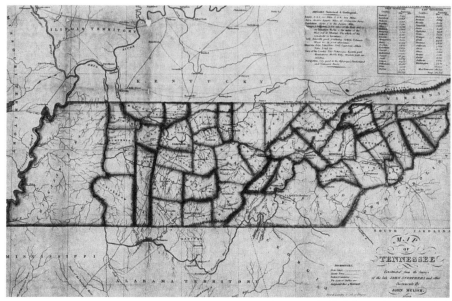

Tennessee in 1818, drawn by John Melish

WILLIAMSON COUNTY

Established 1799; named in honor of Dr. Hugh Williamson

Colonel and Surgeon-General of the North Carolina Militia, a member of the Assembly from Edenton, 1782; later elected to the Continental Congress where he served three terms; he was signer of the Constitution from North Carolina. The county seat is named for his intimate friend, Benjamin Franklin.

TENNESSEE HISTORICAL COMMISSION
Location: U.S. Highway 31 at the Davidson County line, Brentwood

FORREST'S RAID

With two brigades of Cavalry in a widely separated encircling or "Pincher," maneuver on the night of March 24, 1863, Brig. Gen. Nathan Bedford Forrest raided deep behind Federal lines. He completely captured the Federal garrison of 785 officers and men with all valuable stores with loss of but one killed and two wounded.

TENNESSEE HISTORICAL COMMISSION
Location: U.S. Highway 31 at Maryland Way, Brentwood

General Nathan Bedford Forrest

Noble's Corner, a famous Brentwood restaurant

NOBLE'S CORNER

This 5 acres on the corner of Old Hickory Boulevard and Franklin Road was bought by A. H. Noble in 1929. A registered pharmacist, he operated a drug store here for nearly 20 years when the pharmacy was converted to a restaurant by Albert's son Glenn Noble and his wife Iva Lee. The restaurant continued under various managements until 1989. The motel, also built and operated by the Noble family, opened in 1954. Jean Noble Frank built a building on the property that was used for 26 years as Brentwood's post office.

BRENTWOOD HERITAGE AWARD
Location: Corner of Old Hickory Boulevard
and U.S. Highway 31, Brentwood

MOORELAND

Mooreland is built on a land grant to Revolutionary War soldier, General Robert Irvin, upon which his daughter and husband, James Moore, settled in 1807. The original log house stood northeast of Mooreland, which was begun in 1830 by their son, Robert Irvin Moore. Mooreland, an outstanding example of Greek Revival architecture, was used by both sides as a hospital during the Civil War. It was occupied by the Moore family until 1944 and restored by Koger Properties, Inc., in 1985.

ERECTED BY KOGER PROPERTIES, INC., 1987
WILLIAMSON COUNTY HISTORICAL SOCIETY
Location: U.S. Highway 31, Brentwood

Mooreland, an important Greek Revival home, built by Robert Irvin Moore

BRENTWOOD
UNITED METHODIST CHURCH

Founded in 1852, the Brentwood United Methodist Church was located on Frierson Street. The building was destroyed by a storm in 1886, and the church moved to Church Street onto land donated by Mr. and Mrs. Hugh C. Moore. That building was struck by lightning and burned in 1936. It was rebuilt and remained there until the church moved to this site in 1972. A new sanctuary was built here in 1991. It became the largest church in the Tennessee Conference in 1983.

ERECTED BY THE PEP CLUB, 1992
BRENTWOOD HISTORICAL COMMISSION
Location: 309 U.S. Highway 31, Brentwood

*Brentwood United Methodist Church,
built in 1886 (above), circa 1939 (left)*

Johnson Chapel

JOHNSON CHAPEL

Johnson Chapel was established about 1803 on part of Col. Thomas McCrory's property purchased by Maj. John Johnston in 1796. His son Matthew Johnston built the first church here. The land on which that log church stood was deeded to the trustees of the church in 1831, when it was being used by all denominations. Levin Edney, pioneer circuit rider preacher, held the first services here. The first church was destroyed by fire in 1850. This building, erected in 1925, is the third on the site.

ERECTED BY JOHNSON CHAPEL
UNITED METHODIST CHURCH, 1992
WILLIAMSON COUNTY HISTORICAL SOCIETY
Location: High Lea Road, Brentwood

HARDSCUFFLE COMMUNITY

When the slaves were freed in 1865, many of them left local plantations and settled just east of the village of Brentwood. Because of its rocky terrain the area came to be known as Hardscuffle. There African-Americans organized churches, schools, and commercial establishments. The Mt. Lebanon Missionary Baptist Church, founded in 1883, by Rev. Larry Thompson, is still active in the community. Another black church, Brooks Memorial Methodist has moved to another site. After integration the area's black schools were abandoned. The area is now known as Church Street East.

BRENTWOOD HISTORICAL COMMISSION, 1992
Location: Church Street East, Brentwood

Mt. Lebanon Missionary Baptist Church

Typical rock-lined grave

THE STONE BOX INDIAN SITE

When this subdivision was being developed in 1964, ancient Native American remains were discovered. Work was halted until archaelogists explored the site. They found that a Mississippian culture had flourished in a village near here for 500 years between 1200 and 1700 A.D. It was mentioned as "an old Indian town" in the North Carolina land grant to James Crockett. Native Americans of the Mississippian Period had a highly developed culture and buried their dead in "stone box" graves, many of which were found near here. They had mysteriously disappeared by the early 1700s.

BRENTWOOD HISTORICAL COMMISSION
Location: 5215 Seward Drive, Brentwood

Elizabeth McGavock

Lysander McGavock

MIDWAY

Once the camp site of pre-historic Indians, the land on which Midway stands was owned later by James Crockett Sr. of Wythe Co., Va. It was bought from his sons by Lysander McGavock (1800–1855) who married their sister Elizabeth (1795–1862). The present house was completed by a camp-ground and skirmishes were fought in its fields. Midway witnessed the advance and retreat of both armies between Franklin and Nashville in 1864. Its location halfway between those two towns gave the place its name. The house is used (1991) by the Brentwood Country Club.

BRENTWOOD HISTORICAL COMMISSION, 1993
Location: U.S. Highway 31, Brentwood

Scenes of slaves at work

MIDWAY SLAVE CEMETERY

A short distance east of this marker is the site of the Midway Plantation slave cemetery which holds the remains of many of the African Americans who labored on the 1,000 acre plantation in the bonds of slavery during the mid-nineteenth century. By 1850 some 38 slaves toiled on the plantation and through their efforts Lysander McGavock's Midway thrived and boasted 600 acres of improved farmland and produced cash crops of corn and tobacco.

BRENTWOOD HISTORICAL COMMISSION
Location: Murray Lane, Brentwood

Brentwood

Hadleywood

GREEN PASTURES

Green Pastures was part of a North Carolina grant to James Leiper, killed in a raid on Fort Nashboro in 1781. His daughter Sarah Jane married Alexander Smith and settled here. They deeded this land to their daughter Elizabeth, wife of Denney Porterfield Hadley, who in 1839 built a Georgian mansion called Hadleywood. The house was restored by Mason Houghland in the 1930s and acquired by Mr. and Mrs. Cal Turner Jr. in 1992.

BRENTWOOD HISTORICAL COMMISSION
Location: U.S. Highway 31, Brentwood

MOUNTVIEW

The construction of Mountview, begun in the 1850s by William Aurelius and Judith Owen Davis, was completed in 1861. Federal and Confederate armies passed Mountview on their way to Nashville after the Battle of Franklin on Nov. 30, 1864. Two weeks later, after the Battle of Nashville, the Confederates retreated southward past the house in defeat. In 1865, the plantation was sold to Ashley Bascom Rozell, Methodist minister, circuit rider, and planter. Mountview was placed on the National Register of Historical Places in 1986.

BRENTWOOD HISTORICAL COMMISSION, 1993
Location: U.S. Highway 31, Brentwood

Mountview

Owen Chapel Church of Christ

OWEN CHAPEL

Owen Chapel Church of Christ, established July 24, 1857, continued to meet uninterrupted during the Civil War in a log cabin east of this site. The present building was completed in 1867, on land donated by James C. Owen. Early ministers included E. G. Sewell, founder of the Gospel Advocate; William Lipscomb, founder of Lipscomb School, one mile east of this site; and his brother David Lipscomb, founder of David Lipscomb University. The Church continues, stable and active in the affairs of the community.

WILLIAMSON COUNTY HISTORICAL SOCIETY, 1993
Location: U.S. Highway 31, Brentwood

Historical Markers of Williamson County

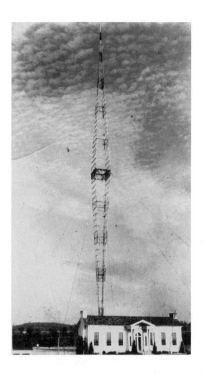

WSM TOWER

This station began operation October 5, 1932, the anniversary of WSM's founding in 1925 by the National Life and Accident Insurance Company of Nashville. WSM-AM operates on a clear channel frequency of 650 kilohertz with power of 50,000 watts. It originated the Grand Ole Opry in 1925 and has continued to broadcast this world famous program on a regular basis. The unique tower, 878 feet high, was the tallest radio tower in the United States at the time of its erection. It sits on a large porcelain insulator and is held vertical by eight insulated steel cables.

WILLIAMSON COUNTY HISTORICAL SOCIETY, 1992
Location: Concord Road, Brentwood

AMERICA'S TALLEST TOWER ~ 878 FEET
WSM *The* **National Life & Accident Insurance Co.. Nashville. Tenn.**

The back and front of a postcard of a familiar Brentwood landmark, WSM Tower

*Lipscomb Elementary School,
before 1958 (above), before 1949 (right)*

LIPSCOMB ELEMENTARY SCHOOL

The school was founded as a private academy in the 1860s by Professor William Lipscomb, brother of David Lipscomb, founder of David Lipscomb University. Students were attracted to the school from the local area as well as from other parts of the state. In the late 1800s it became part of the Williamson County public school system and operated as a two room school until 1949 when a new building was erected. It burned in 1958 and was replaced. The present facility was completed in 1993.

ERECTED BY ALUMNI, STUDENTS, AND FRIENDS
BRENTWOOD HISTORICAL COMMISSION
WILLIAMSON COUNTY HISTORICAL SOCIETY
Location: 8011 Concord Road, Brentwood

Isola Bella

ISOLA BELLA

This house was built about 1840 by James and Naricissa Merritt Johnston on land that had belonged to David Johnston, pioneer in Middle Tennessee and grandfather of the builder. During the Civil War the Johnston home was passed by Confederate and Federal armies after the Battles of Franklin and Nashville. It served as headquarters of Gen. John B. Hood and his staff before the conflict at Nashville and as a hospital after that ill-fated battle on Dec. 15–16.

FAMILY OF DAVE A. ALEXANDER, 1990
WILLIAMSON COUNTY HISTORICAL SOCIETY
Location: 1112 U.S. Highway 31, Brentwood

TENNESSEE BAPTIST
CHILDREN'S HOME

On May 5, 1891 a committee assembled by Mrs. Georgia Eastman met to organize the "Tennessee Baptist Orphans' Home." The home became a reality Oct. 13, 1891 when by-laws were adopted, application made for incorporation, and the former Delaware Hotel in Nashville rented. The Rev. T. T. Thompson was the first staff member. Four children were received the next month. The home became part of the Tennessee Baptist Convention in 1894. Because more space was needed, ground was broken near here April 15, 1911 for a new building on what was then a 75-acre site. The home's name was changed in 1953 to "Tennessee Baptist Children's Home." Group homes replaced dormitories between 1971 and 1974.

WILLIAMSON COUNTY HISTORICAL SOCIETY, 1999
Location: U.S. Highway 31, Brentwood

Tennessee Baptist Children's Home campus, which includes David Johnston Cemetery, circa 1948

DAVID JOHNSTON CEMETERY

On this campus is located the family cemetery of Revolutionary War soldier David Johnston, who came to Williamson County from Mecklenburg, N.C. by 1807. Those known to be buried here are David Johnston (1745–1829), Elizabeth Johnston (1747–1827), Robert Johnston (1775–1827), Rachel Johnston (1782–1864), David Johnston Jr., Carrie Johnston (1803–1824), Esau Johnston (1836–1863), Henry C. Johnston, Fannie C. Johnston (1840–1864), Rachel Johnston (1830–1848), William W. Ford, James Polk Reed (1844–1909), and Dallas Reed (1842–1920). There are also a large number of unknown graves in the cemetery.

WILLIAMSON COUNTY HISTORICAL SOCIETY, 1999
Location: U.S. Highway 31, Brentwood

Hood's Retreat

Falling back to this locality from its position along Little Harpeth River, Lee's Corps, with Chalmer's cavalry division, stood off the attacks of Wood's IV Corps and Wilson's cavalry until outflanked on both sides. They then followed Hood's retreating army south through Franklin.

TENNESSEE HISTORICAL COMMISSION
Location: U.S. Highway 31, Brentwood, at the foot of Holly Tree Gap Hill

Holly Tree Gap

These Pioneers
George Neely, William McEwen,
Andrew Goff, David McEwen
passed through
Holly Tree Gap
March 1798

PLACED BY OLD GLORY CHAPTER
DAUGHTERS OF THE AMERICAN REVOLUTION
ASSISTED BY DESCENDANTS OF THESE MEN, 1925
Location: U.S. Highway 31 at Holly Tree Gap, Brentwood

Boiling Springs Academy, 1833

THE BOILING SPRINGS SITE

Once five significant mounds marked the site of an ancient Indian village here. The mounds were between Little Harpeth River and a branch of the Boiling Springs. When the four burial mounds were excavated in 1895 and again in 1920, artifacts were found dating back to the Mississippian Period of Indian culture in Tennessee. Relics from the second excavation were placed in the Smithsonian Institution in Washington. The ceremonial mound by Boiling Springs Academy was left undisturbed.

ERECTED BY BRENTWOOD ROTARY CLUB, 1976
Location: Moores Lane, Brentwood

Forge Seat, Crockett home on Wilson Pike

FORGE SEAT

Forge Seat was built in 1808 by Samuel Crockett III, one of a large family of Crocketts who settled on extensive tracts of land in this area during the late 1700s. This house took its name from an iron forge on the property where Crockett and his son, Andrew Crockett, made rifles, which were identified by their fine craftsmanship and the initials "S. & A. C." engraved on the barrels. Andrew Jackson stopped here on the way to the Indian wars to arm his soldiers with Crockett rifles. Samuel and Andrew Crockett and other family members are buried in this cemetery.

WILLIAMSON COUNTY HISTORICAL SOCIETY, 1993
Location: Wilson Pike at Crockett Road, Brentwood

Andrew Crockett 1745–1821
Revolutionary War Land Grant
Crockett's Home "Forge Seat" Across Road

BY CLARENDON CHAPTER TN SOCIETY
COLONIAL DAMES XVII CENTURY
Location: Crockett Cemetery, Wilson Pike and Crockett Road, Brentwood

Historical Markers of Williamson County

KNOX-CROCKETT HOUSE

This house was built by Major Andrew Crockett, planter and gunsmith, who came here with his family in the late 1700s. He was the ancestor of several Crockett families who lived in the area. The house is built on a Revolutionary War Grant to Major Crockett.

The oldest part is a log cabin built in the late 1790s. The newest section was built in the mid 1800s. The house was first restored under the direction of Dr. Mack Wayne Craig. Further restoration was done by Robert C. Williams who bought the house in 1991.

BRENTWOOD HISTORICAL COMMISSION
WILLIAMSON COUNTY HISTORICAL SOCIETY, 1994
Location: 8230 Wikle Road, Brentwood

Early Crockett home near the Little Harpeth River

Portrait of young Reverend Green Hill, Methodist pioneer minister

GREEN HILL

This Revolutionary War officer and Methodist leader settled and built his home here in 1799. He was influential in establishing Methodism on the Tennessee frontier and founded the Liberty Methodist Church one mile east. The Western Conference of the Methodist Episcopal church of 1808, held at his home, was attended by Bishop Francis Asbury and newly elected Bishop William McKendree. The Hill family cemetery a short distance south and near the site of his home is maintained as a shrine by the Tennessee Conference of the United Methodist Church.

ERECTED BY GREEN HILL'S DESCENDANTS
WILLIAMSON COUNTY HISTORICAL SOCIETY, 1994
Location: Concord Road at Green Hills Boulevard, Brentwood

GREEN HILL SHRINE

Green Hill (Nov. 2, 1741–Sept. 11, 1826) moved from North Carolina to the large plantation of which this is a center in 1799. Hill was a Revolutionary War Colonel, generous philanthropist, and a Methodist preacher for over 50 years. On Oct. 1–7, 1808, he entertained the ninth session of the Western Conference of the Methodist Church at this place. The cemetery nearby, in which Hill and his family are buried, was given by 58 of his descendants to the Tennessee Conference of the Methodist Church on June 25, 1960, and was accepted as a Methodist shrine.

TENNESSEE HISTORICAL COMMISSION
Location: Green Hill Cemetery in Liberty Downs Subdivision, Brentwood

Resting place of the Green Hill family

COTTONPORT

Cottonport stands on the site of Mayfield Station, a fort constructed as protection from Indian raids. Built on the site of an old Indian town, the station was attacked by Indians in 1788. John Frost, later a captain in the War of 1812, came here from Newberry, South Carolina in the early 1800s. While building his brick home he lived in a log house believed to be the present smoke house. With the addition of a cotton gin, general store, grist mill and post office, Cottonport became the commercial center for the surrounding community.

BRENTWOOD HISTORICAL COMMISSION
WILLIAMSON COUNTY HISTORICAL SOCIETY, 1994
Location: 9304 Old Smyrna Road, Brentwood

Cottonport, early site of Mayfield Station

Sneed Acres, drawn by Bill Vantrease

SNEED ACRES

Sneed Acres was established as a plantation in 1799 by James Sneed (1764–1853) and wife Bethenia Harden Perkins Sneed (1770–1853). They came to this area from Halifax County, Virginia. Three original buildings remain on this site with a portion of the old log home being incorporated into present home. Three sons built homes nearby: Windy Hill ca. 1825 by Constantine, Brentvale ca. 1830 by William Temple and Foxview ca.1835 by Alexander Ewing. Sneed family members are buried in the cemetery just south of here. Dr. William J. Sneed, grandson of pioneer James, was one of the founders of Meharry Medical College.

ERECTED BY INTERNATIONAL ASSOCIATION OF SNEEDS
WILLIAMSON COUNTY HISTORICAL SOCIETY
Location: 9207 Old Smyrna Road, Brentwood

Part II
EASTERN
WILLIAMSON
COUNTY

<table>
<tr><td>1 – Nolensville</td><td>9 – Triune</td></tr>
<tr><td>2 – Nolensville Cemetery</td><td>10 – Bostick Female</td></tr>
<tr><td>3 – Nolensville United</td><td>Academy</td></tr>
<tr><td>Methodist Church</td><td>11 – Trinity Church</td></tr>
<tr><td>4 – Sherwood Green</td><td>12 – Rock Hill</td></tr>
<tr><td>5 – Wheeler's Raid Around</td><td>13 – Arrington</td></tr>
<tr><td>Rosecrans</td><td>14 – Daniel M. Robinson</td></tr>
<tr><td>6 – Dewitt Smith Jobe</td><td>15 – Newton Cannon</td></tr>
<tr><td>7 – Triune United Methodist</td><td>16 – College Grove</td></tr>
<tr><td>Church</td><td>17 – College Grove</td></tr>
<tr><td>8 – Wilson Creek Primitive</td><td>Methodist Church</td></tr>
<tr><td>Baptist Church</td><td>18 – Ogilvie Farm</td></tr>
</table>

96

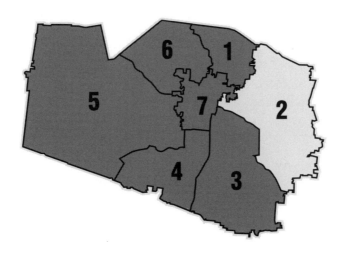

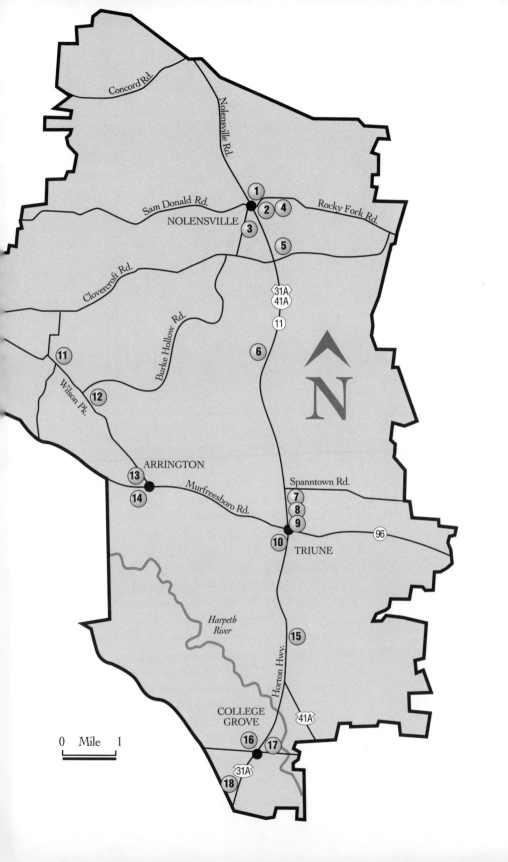

The village of Nolensville, circa 1910

NOLENSVILLE

William Nolen purchased the portion of a land grant to Jason Thompson on which Nolensville, named for him, was later built. In the early 1800s a large migration from Rockingham County, N.C. brought the Adams, Allen, Barnes, Cyrus, Fields, Glenn, Irion, Johnson, Peay, Scales, Taylor, Vernon, Wisener and other families to the area. Built along Mill Creek, the town was incorporated in 1839. Foraging and skirmishing took place here during the Civil War, Gen. John Wharton's Confederate Cavalry unit was stationed in the town briefly and Gen. Joseph Wheeler's command captured a Union Supply train here on December 30, 1862. Several buildings in the business district burned in 1953. Nolensville was re-incorporated in 1996.

WILLIAMSON COUNTY HISTORICAL SOCIETY, 1999
Location: U.S. Highway 31–A

Historical Markers of Williamson County

Waller Funeral Home, Williamson County's oldest family business

NOLENSVILLE CEMETERY

This cemetery was begun in 1899 by J. W. Williams on land bought from Isaac Neely. The mid-section began in 1917 as the S. G. Jenkins cemetery. J. W. Williams bought adjoining land in 1925 and expanded the Jenkins cemetery. The Cemetery Association was formed and the Perpetual Care Fund set up in 1975, with J. B. Ozburn, Frank H. Waller, Mattie Sue and Walter D. Ragsdale, Maurice Williams, Will Brittain, J. T. Williams, Thomas Scales, Stanley Fly and Vance Little as Trustees.

NOLENSVILLE CEMETERY ASSOCIATION, 1998
Location: Clovercroft Road

Nolensville United Methodist Church, circa 1900

NOLENSVILLE
UNITED METHODIST CHURCH

This church was founded in 1837 as Mt. Olivet Methodist Episcopal Church, South. Original trustees were Joseph Critchlow, John Hay, Benjamin Johnson, Benjamin King, John Matthews, Phillip Owen, and Nathaniel Owen. Originally, the church was located on Williams Road on land purchased in 1839 from John Hay and Samuel Bittick. In 1858, the congregation moved to the Nolensville Turnpike about one-half mile south of this site. The second church building was heavily damaged during the Civil War. On September 14, 1894, land was purchased here and this building, with its tall steeple and church bell which is rung every Sunday morning, was erected. Over time, stained glass windows were installed in memory of faithful members.

WILLIAMSON COUNTY HISTORICAL SOCIETY, 1997
Location: U.S. Highway 31–A

Home to the Greens since 1803

SHERWOOD GREEN

Sherwood Green (1766–1840) came to Tennessee in the late 1700s, from Warren County, N.C. as a member of a team of surveyors charged with surveying North Carolina Revolutionary War grants. The team was headed by his father-in-law, Col. William Christmas, who in 1803 became Tennessee Surveyor General and Entry Taker. Green selected this site to make his home and brought his family here in 1803. He built this two-story log house, owned 1689 acres, and was active in the Methodist Church and the Masonic Order. He rests in the nearby cemetery beside his wife, Martha Christmas Green and other family members.

WILLIAMSON COUNTY HISTORICAL SOCIETY
Location: Rocky Fork Road

WHEELER'S RAID AROUND ROSECRANS

U.S. General W. S. Rosecrans

Dec. 30, 1862. After destroying a sizable wagon train at Rock Springs, about six miles northeast Wheeler's Confederate raiders, late in the afternoon here capture about 200 prisoners, destroyed a wagon train and took with them a number of ambulances. They then moved southwestward, to bivouac about two miles north of Arrington.

TENNESSEE HISTORICAL COMMISSION
Location: U.S. Highway 31–A, south of Nolensville

DEWITT SMITH JOBE

Dewitt Smith Jobe

A member of Coleman's Scouts, C.S.A., he was captured in a cornfield about 1/2 mi. W. Aug. 29, 1864, by a patrol from the 115th Ohio Cav. Swallowing his dispatches, he was mutilated and tortured to make him reveal their contents. Refusing, he was dragged to death behind a galloping horse. He is buried in the family cemetery 6 miles northeast.

TENNESSEE HISTORICAL COMMISSION
Location: U.S. Highway 31–A, south of Nolensville

Historical Markers of Williamson County

TRIUNE
UNITED METHODIST CHURCH

The Triune United Methodist Church's origin goes back to King's Chapel, organized ca.1815 a mile west. A brick building was built here in 1849 on the then-new highway. The church was named Triune and the village, previously known as Hardeman Cross Roads, soon took the same name. Burned by Union troops in 1863, trustees James A. Bostick, Sam Perkins, James M. Peebles, Isaac Page, Frank Hawkins, H. A. Roper, W. H. Matthews, J. H. Glenn, and John Page, voted to rebuild on the old site. The present church was dedicated in 1874, the same year a cemetery was opened in the church yard.

IN MEMORY OF JOHN U. WILSON
WILLIAMSON COUNTY HISTORICAL SOCIETY, 1995
Location: U.S. Highway 31–A, Triune

Triune Church, 1874

Williamson County's oldest church building

WILSON CREEK
PRIMITIVE BAPTIST CHURCH

This church was organized on October 13, 1804 with forty-six members, including fourteen African-Americans. Early families to worship here were Clayton, Davis, Fleming, Hill, Hyde, Jordan, McKnight, McFadden, and Pate. The site was donated by John D. Hill, the congregation's first clerk. The brick church, which is the oldest meeting house in the county, was built in 1816. Elder Garner McConnico (1771–1833) served as the first minister. During the Civil War the building was used as a barracks by Union troops. The names of soldiers and their regiments were inscribed on pews and columns.

WILLIAMSON COUNTY HISTORICAL SOCIETY, 1997
Location: U.S. Highway 31–A, Triune

Perkins family on the porch of Westview (above) and Hardeman Academy (right)

TRIUNE

This village dates from about 1800 and was first called Hardeman Cross Roads. After 1849 it took the name of the Methodist Church and became known as Triune. Prior to the Civil War, Triune was a flourishing center of commerce and agriculture. Known for its fine schools and stately homes, the Triune district's four academies attracted students from afar. Hardeman Academy, built one-fourth mile west in 1831, burned in 1904. Westview, the elegant antebellum mansion of Samuel Perkins, stood about a half mile south until it burned in 1927. From 1863 until 1865 Triune was occupied by Union soldiers who destroyed churches, schools, and homes. At least fifteen military engagements were fought here.

IN MEMORY OF DR. GARNER M. JORDAN (1838–1908)
WILLIAMSON COUNTY HISTORICAL SOCIETY, 1999
Location: U.S. Highway 31–A, Triune

BOSTICK FEMALE ACADEMY

Dr. Jonathan Bostick, a resident of Triune who died in 1872 at his cotton plantation in Mississippi, bequeathed the funds for this school. It was his desire to replace the famed Porter Female Academy, burned by Union soldiers in 1863, and to maintain the tradition of fine schools for boys and girls in the Triune district. The money arrived in 1891 after a long delay. John S. Claybrooke, the only trustee named in Bostick's will still living, used it to buy eleven acres from the Samuel Perkins estates and had this handsome edifice built. Bostick Female Academy's first session was held in 1893. After Hardeman Academy burned in 1904, this building served as the Triune Public School until 1949. It is now a private residence.

WILLIAMSON COUNTY HISTORICAL SOCIETY, 1999
Location: U.S. Highway, 31–A, Triune

Triune School, circa 1911

Trinity Church

TRINITY CHURCH

This United Methodist Church was an outgrowth of Mt. Zion Methodist Church, established about 1840 in Burke Hollow near the Tom Page house. Mt. Zion was destroyed in 1863 by Union soldiers who used its materials for a signal station on Daddy's Knob. Trinity Church was organized in 1865 with most of its founders being former Confederate soldiers. On this site in 1869, a two-story brick building was completed; a school and Masonic lodge were located above the church sanctuary. After damage by a tornado in 1897, the church was rebuilt on the same stone foundation with original handmade bricks. The second floor was not rebuilt. In 1909, the bell tower and the north and east walls were damaged by a tornado.

WILLIAMSON COUNTY HISTORICAL SOCIETY, 1997
Location: Wilson Pike, Trinity Community

Rock Hill's store, circa 1896

ROCK HILL

With the completion in 1844 of the Harpeth Turnpike, now known as Wilson Pike, the hamlet of Rock Hill grew and became the commercial center for a large area. The original store and post office building was located 350 yards south at the driveway entrance to the George Pollard house. Beyond the store, near the Pollard-Tulloss graveyard, was a steam cotton gin operated by Pollard and Tom Tulloss. The turnpike's southernmost tollgate was located at the junction with Starnes' Mill (Shag Rag) Road. Near the entrance to Burke Hollow Road were a blacksmith shop and sawmill. At this site in 1896, Rock Hill's second store was built. Operated for many years by S. R. Lamb, it burned in 1954.

WILLIAMSON COUNTY HISTORICAL SOCIETY, 1998
Location: Wilson Pike between Burke Hollow and Shag Rag Roads

Williamson County's first shopping center

ARRINGTON

The early settlement of "Petersburg" was granted a post office in 1858. At that time, the village's name was changed to Arrington for the nearby creek. Among the early families were Buchanan, Couch, Crockett, Duff, King, Morris, Paschall, Price, Roberts, and Sayers. Four churches were established: Bellview Cumberland Presbyterian (1852), Hopewell A.M.E. (1876), Patton's Chapel A.M.E. (1882), and First Baptist (1968). Arrington School and Patton's Chapel School were located on Cox Road. The original store and post office were on the west corner of Wilson Pike and Murfreesboro Road. When the railroad arrived in 1914, a depot was built. At one time, the village had two stores, a livery stable, grist mill, and blacksmith shop.

WILLIAMSON COUNTY HISTORICAL SOCIETY, 1999
Location: Highway 96 at the fire station

Daniel M. Robison,
Williamson County trustee, state historian

DANIEL M. ROBISON

1893–1970

Born 1/2 mile southwest, Dr. Robison spent his boyhood in this community. He taught at Battle Ground Academy, Memphis State College, and Vanderbilt University. While he was State Librarian and Archivist, a new library and archives building was constructed. The state historical marker program was begun by the Tennessee Historical Commission during his service as its chairman. He compiled biographical directories of Tennessee Legislators and was serving as State Historian at the time of his death.

TENNESSEE HISTORICAL COMMISSION
Location: Highway 96, Arrington

The home (above), destroyed by fire in 1987, of Governor Newton Cannon (inset)

NEWTON CANNON

0.7 miles. The grave of this combat veteran and statesman is on the land to which his father, a Revolutionary veteran, brought his family from North Carolina in 1791. In addition to his distinguished military record, he was twice a member of Congress and twice governor of Tennessee.

TENNESSEE HISTORICAL COMMISSION
Location: U.S. Highway 31–A and Talliaferro Road, Kirkland

COLLEGE GROVE

Once called Harpeth, then Poplar Grove, this area was settled about 1800 by the Allison, Cannon, Ogilvie, and Wilson families. Home to Congressman Meredith Gentry and William Demonbreun, son of pioneer Timothy Demonbreun, the town's name was changed to College Grove when a post office was established in 1860. Other pioneer families were Allen, Covington, Dobson, Haley, Hughes, McCord, Patton, Rogers, Scales, Seay, and Webb. Poplar Grove Cumberland Presbyterian Church and Cary and Winn Male Academy stood on land donated by James Allison in 1859. Stage coaches operated here until 1905. The Bank of College Grove opened in 1911.

WILLIAMSON COUNTY HISTORICAL SOCIETY, 1997
Location: U.S. Highway 31–A, College Grove

The Nashville-Chapel Hill stagecoach stopped in College Grove

College Grove Methodist Church, built in 1888

COLLEGE GROVE METHODIST CHURCH

On March 31, 1860, Dr. Samuel Webb deeded the land for College Grove Methodist Episcopal Church South and a seminary for young ladies. The present Victorian structure was erected in 1888 by T. G. Slate. Two pioneer circuit riders who served here were Jeremiah W. Cullom and J. B. McFerrin. In 1955, the church became a full station. Among the families listed on the church's early register are Critchlow, Demonbreun, Drumright, Glenn, Haley, Jordan, Long, Maxwell, Miller, Neeley, Ogilvie, and Patton. Memorial windows were added in 1952 and 1984. The steeple was erected in 1983 in honor of the Joe C. Bellenfant family.

IN MEMORY OF BEATRICE OGILVIE
WILLIAMSON COUNTY HISTORICAL SOCIETY, 1999
Location: U.S. Highway 31–A, College Grove

Ogilvie Farm

This property was settled by William and Mary Harris Ogilvie, who came to this area via ox wagons from Granville County, N.C. during the late 1790s. Their nine children— Harris, Sarah, Smith, Kimbrough, John, William, Patty, Richard, and Nancy—also settled here and nearby. The family descends from the ancient Ogilvy Clan of Angus, Scotland, and had farmed American soil since early colonial days. The original 1800-era log house and the adjacent Ogilvie family cemetery, established in 1807, are listed on the National Register of Historical Places. In 1998, the Ogilvie place was one of the state's oldest farms remaining within the same family throughout its history.

IN MEMORY OF PAUL OGILVIE
WILLIAMSON COUNTY HISTORICAL SOCIETY, 1998
Location: U.S. Highway 31–A, south of College Grove

Ogilvie Farm slave cabin (left) and springhouse (above)

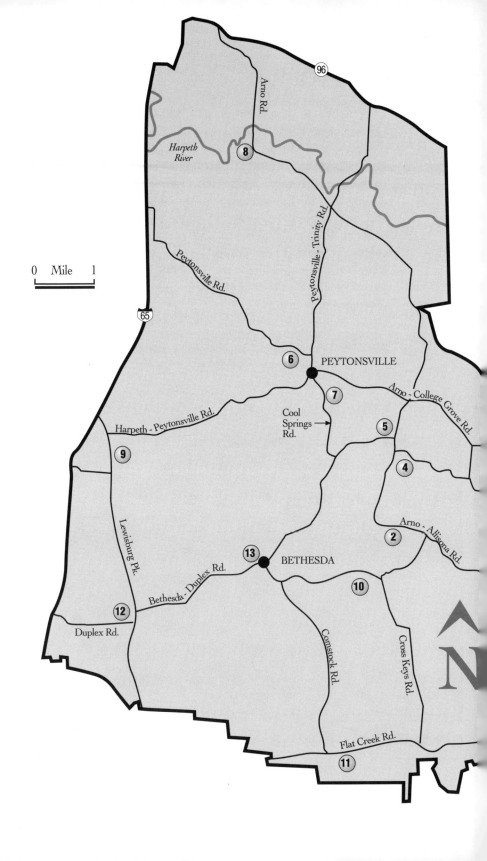

Part III

SOUTHEASTERN WILLIAMSON COUNTY

1 – Riggs Cross Roads
2 – The Cove
3 – Owen Hill
4 – Rucker Cemetery
5 – Arno
6 – Peytonsville
7 – Sam and Kirk McGee
8 – Epworth United

Methodist Church
9 – New Hope Presbyterian Church
10 – Cross Keys
11 – Moses Steele Cemetery
12 – Mount Carmel/Duplex
13 – Bethesda

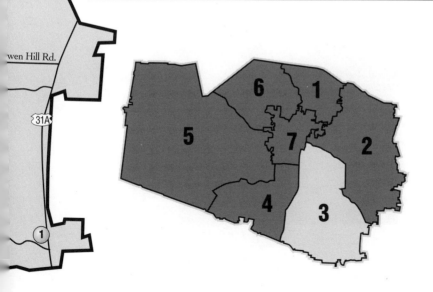

RIGGS CROSS ROADS

Located 110 yards west at crossing of Fishing Ford or Riggs Rd., oldest traveled thoroughfare in Middle Tennessee, and old Columbia or Flat Creek Rd. Old village compound consisted of a brick house, post office, blacksmith shop, and store on about 1000 acres expanded by Gideon Riggs from the 555 acres recorded in 1811 by his father, David Riggs from North Carolina. Scene of Civil War Headquarters of General Forrest. Gideon married three times each with descendants — Mary Reynolds: Ogilvie; Sophia Campbell: Haley; Mary Catherine Holden: Brittain, Duggan, Fuller, and Riggs.

ERECTED BY DESCENDANTS, 1985
WILLIAMSON COUNTY HISTORICAL SOCIETY
Location: U.S. Highway 31–A at Riggs Road

Portrait of Gideon Riggs

The Robert Graham family (above)and Harpeth Lick Cumberland Presbyterian Church (inset)

THE COVE

Shadowed on the southwest by Pull-Tight Hill and bisected by Arno Road, the Cove was home to the Biggers, Bizzell, Clendenin, Connell, Crafton, Creswell, Farrar, Graham, Ladd, Rickman, Simmons, Skinner, Watson, White, and Wilson families. On May 10, 1863, the political complexion of the area changed when eight Confederate soldiers murdered Will Biggers, a medically discharged Confederate soldier whose brother was in the Union army. As a result of this misdeed, the Cove became a Republican island in a Democratic county. Harpeth Lick Cumberland Presbyterian Church, est. 1833, and Beech Grove United Methodist Church, est. 1878, remain active congregations. Simmons Hill School, built in 1898, closed in 1947.

WILLIAMSON COUNTY HISTORICAL SOCIETY, 1999
Location: Arno Road between Arno and Allisona

OWEN HILL

Once a thriving community, Owen Hill was home to Peter, Richard, and Greenberry Owen, pioneer tobacconists, who came to Williamson County in 1817. Confederate surgeon Dr. Urban G. Owen began practicing medicine here in 1859. In 1850 this site upon which was built a two story lodge and academy, was sold by George C. Kinnard to James S. Ogilvie, C. M. Comstock, J. B. Wilson, of Owen Hill Lodge No. 172 F & A. M. and Rev. Wm. Burns, W. N. Haley, James P. Allison, E. L. Jordan, J. B. Wilson, and Johnson Jordan, Owen Hill Female Academy trustees. In 1885 the lodge moved to Allisona, and in 1955 to College Grove. Owen Hill's identity faded in 1952 with the closing of Allison School, a school for black children since the 1860s.

IN MEMORY OF JOHN U. WILSON
WILLIAMSON COUNTY HISTORICAL SOCIETY, 1998
Location: Owen Hill Road

Owen Hill Lodge No. 172, Free and Accepted Masons, before 1885

Alonzo DeAlvarado Rucker

RUCKER CEMETERY

The cemetery, which had its beginning in 1826, is located one-half mile south. William Rucker Sr. (1760–1826), a Revolutionary War veteran, was the first person buried in the cemetery. Also buried there are his son, William Rucker Jr. (1791–1868), a color-bearer in the War of 1812; Col. Octavius Claiborne Hatcher, a Mexican War veteran; Capt. William Pillow Rucker, C.S.A., who was killed at the Battle of Fort Donelson in 1863; Captain Rucker's two brothers, Alonzo DeAlvarado Rucker and John S. Rucker; and a brother-in-law, Robert Archer Jordan. The last three men served in Company D, 20th Tennessee Infantry Regiment, C.S.A. The cemetery is maintained by The Historical Rucker Family Cemetery Association.

WILLIAMSON COUNTY HISTORICAL SOCIETY, 1998
Location: Owen Hill Road

Syl and Van Smithson at E. K. Smithson's store, Arno

ARNO

Arno was named by a U.S. Postal official for the Italian river. The name has long outlasted the post office which closed in 1908. Once located at this crossroads leading to College Grove, Peytonsville, Allisona, and Rudderville were country stores operated by E. K. Smithson, Earl Culberson, Eugene "Red" Jordan, and Milton Ryan. Arno had a public school from 1893 until 1947. Wesley Chapel Methodist, originally established in 1834, moved to its present location on Arno Road in 1907. Historic community names include Burns, Graham, Hatcher, Jordan, Low, Miller, Petway, Pinkston, Rucker, Sledge, and White. Dr. W. W. Graham, Rev. Wm. Burns, and Magistrate E. K. "Lige" Smithson were prominent citizens.

WILLIAMSON COUNTY HISTORICAL SOCIETY, 1999
Location: Crossroads of Arno and Peytonsville-College Grove Roads

Historical Markers of Williamson County

Church of Christ established in 1884 (above) and N. N. Smithson home (inset)

PEYTONSVILLE

Once called Snatchit, Peytonsville had a post office from 1835 until 1908. Early settlers included Revolutionary War veterans Daniel Crenshaw and John Secrest and the children of Revolutionary War soldier John S. Smithson. Area churches include Cool Springs Primitive Baptist Church, est. in 1881; Peytonsville Methodist Church, now Chapel of Hope, est. 1851; Peytonsville Church of Christ, est. 1884; and Peytonsville Baptist Church, est. 1959. The public school closed in 1962. Historic names include: Gee, Glenn, Gosey, Gray, Harrison, Helm, Holland, Johnson, Mangrum, Meeks, Nevils, Reid, Smithson, Tomlin, and Vaden. To the south lies "Little Texas," home to the Bennett, Garner, Guffee, McGee, Poteete, and Veach families.

WILLIAMSON COUNTY HISTORICAL SOCIETY, 1999
Location: Intersection of Peytonsville and Gosey Hill Roads

SAM AND KIRK McGEE

These accomplished brothers were born near here in the 1890s. Both learned to play banjos from their father and performed with him at local dances. They became accomplished musicians, Sam on the guitar and Kirk on the fiddle, first appearing on the Grand Ole Opry in 1926 with Uncle Dave Macon's Fruit Jar Drinkers. The same year the "Boys from Tennessee" made their first recordings in New York. They performed during the 1930s as the Dixieliners and teamed up with Bill Monroe's Blue Grass Boys in the 1940s. Because of their purity of style, their popularity increased in the 1950s when they played many college campuses and folk festivals. Sam and Kirk McGee performed on the Opry until their deaths in 1975 and 1983.

WILLIAMSON COUNTY HISTORICAL SOCIETY, 1999
Location: Cool Springs Road

Kirk and Sam McGee, country music legends

Historical Markers of Williamson County

Epworth United Methodist Church, a country church built in 1910

EPWORTH
UNITED METHODIST CHURCH

This Church, dedicated in 1910, was formed by the union of two earlier churches, Thomas Church (1853) and North's Chapel (1866). Land for the new church was given by Jesse A. and Mittie Toon Pierce. The chancel rail from the old Thomas Church and the pulpit from North's Chapel were incorporated in the new building which was erected in 1909. The Good Shepherd window was dedicated to Beverly B. and Sara D. Nolen Toon, and W. M. Nolen. The Toons' home, Riverside, still stands across Arno Road. In 1952 Sunday school rooms were added. The next year Epworth became a charge and a parsonage was built on land given by Mary Hatcher. A large fellowship hall and educational annex were added in 1987.

WILLIAMSON COUNTY HISTORICAL SOCIETY, 1997
Location: Arno Road at Millview

New Hope Presbyterian Church, built in 1869

New Hope Presbyterian Church

Rev. Duncan Brown organized the Presbyterians in the Duck River Ridge region in 1806. The first log church, called Ridge Meeting House, was erected one mile south of here four years later; this was the first church south of Franklin in Williamson County. The congregation moved into a new frame building in 1829 and possibly changed the name to New Hope then. The third and present church was built in 1869.

TENNESSEE HISTORICAL COMMISSION
Location: Lewisburg Pike, south of Franklin

Historical Markers of Williamson County

CROSS KEYS

Laban Hartley Jr. built a stone house here ca. 1818 and operated a tavern for which this community was named. Mt. Pisgah, located 1/2 mile to the s.w., was used as a reference point by surveyors when creating the 1783 Military Reservation line. Pull Tight Hill, which received its name because of having to "pull tight" when crossing it, is the highest point in the county, rising 1,256 feet above sea level. Two churches, Mt. Zion Methodist U.S.A. (1869–1994) and Cross Keys Baptist, est.1954, are area landmarks. Choctaw School operated from 1871 to 1946. Joe D. Trice opened a store at this crossroads in 1910. Other early families include Anderson, Bigger, Crafton, Creswell, Giles, Hargrove, Henderson, Irvin, McCall, Skinner, and Walton.

WILLIAMSON COUNTY HISTORICAL SOCIETY, 1999
Location: Cross Keys Road

Choctaw School, closed in 1946

MOSES STEELE CEMETERY

This historic cemetery is the resting place for an impressive number of Revolutionary War soldiers. Thought to be buried here are the remains of these American patriots who fought in our War of Independence: David Gillespie (1761–1835) of N.C., Thomas Gillespie (1755–1830) of N.C., Isaac Gillespie (1750–1826) of N.C., Bennett Hargrove (1764–1842) of Va., Laban Hartley (1742–1843) of Md., Sherwood Smith (1761–1851) of Va., Zachariah Smith (1757–1840) of N.C., and Moses Steele (17 —1844). In 1808, Steele, a Mecklenburg County, N.C. planter, bought 225 acres of the 4,000 acre land grant of Thomas Gillespie. Steele gave part of that land for this cemetery.

WILLIAMSON COUNTY HISTORICAL SOCIETY, 1996
Location: Flat Creek Road

Traditional Scottish stacked-stone grave of Laban Hartley

Mount Carmel Cumberland Presbyterian Church, built in 1913

MOUNT CARMEL/DUPLEX

In 1827 Allen Bugg deeded 3 1/2 acres of the "old camp-grounds" to W. W. Bond, T. E. Kirkpatrick, Clement Wall and Newton Wall, trustees of Mt. Carmel Church, the first Cumberland Presbyterian Church in the county. The building, burned by Union soldiers, was rebuilt after the Civil War only to be so damaged by a 1913 storm that it was torn down and the present church erected. Mt. Carmel School, next to the church, closed in 1951. The Lewisburg Turnpike tollgate was located a few yards to the north. The community adopted its present name, Duplex, in honor of John Lee's famous pacer, which set a world's record for the mile. Early area families were Crutcher, Lee, McCord, Oden, Padgett, Short, Stephens, Thompson, and Warren.

WILLIAMSON COUNTY HISTORICAL SOCIETY, 1998
Location: Lewisburg Pike and Duplex Road

Pleasant Scales's store (above) and Bethesda School, 1936 (inset)

BETHESDA

Bethesda is a Biblical name meaning "House of Mercy." Early family names in the community included Alexander, Bond, Blythe, Grigsby, Irvin, Sprott, Steele, and Waddey. Beloved area physicians were Drs. Blythe, Core, Eggleston, and Bennett. Gone but once thriving were Chrisman's broom factory, Mosley's sawmill, Scales' store and post office, and Waddey's chair factory. Masonic Lodge 201 was organized in 1830. The community's first two school buildings were at the crossroads before the school moved to this hill in 1936. The Methodist Church, organized in 1832, moved to its present location in 1960. The Presbyterian Church was organized and built in 1879.

IN MEMORY OF JAMES W. BOND AND LEO GRIGSBY BOND
WILLIAMSON COUNTY HISTORICAL SOCIETY, 1998
Location: Bethesda Community Center

Bethesda School, 1900–1927 (top), 1928–1935 (bottom)

Part IV
SOUTHERN
WILLIAMSON
COUNTY

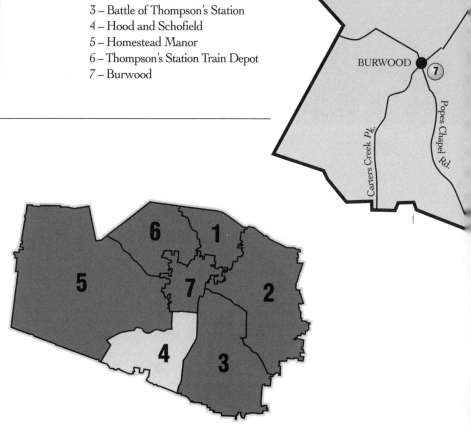

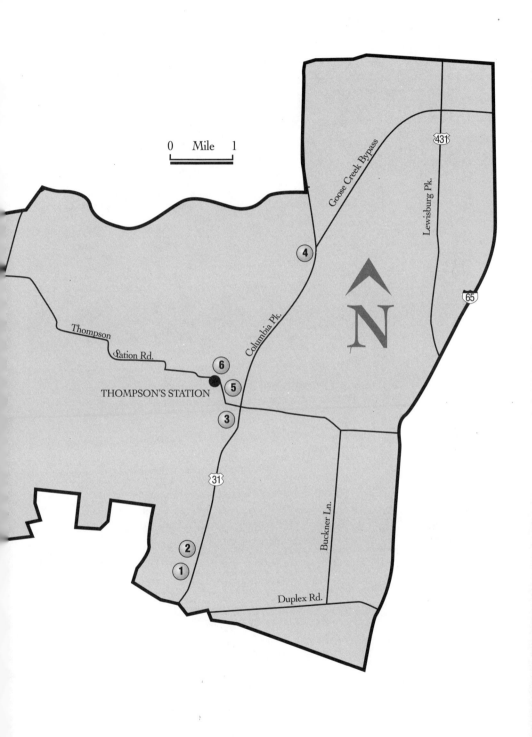

0 Mile 1

Goose Creek Bypass

431

Lewisburg Pk.

65

④

Columbia Pk.

Thompson
Station Rd.

⑥

⑤

THOMPSON'S STATION

③

N

31

Buckner Ln.

②

①

Duplex Rd.

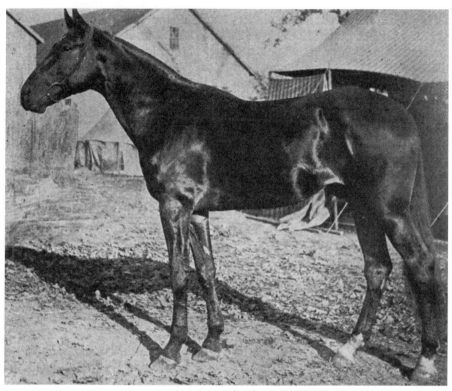

Star Pointer, first horse in harness to break the two-minute mile

STAR POINTER

Foaled 1889, in a barn 200 yards west, he was the son of Brown Hal and Sweepstakes. His owner was Capt. Henry P. Pointer, who also bred Hal Pointer. Pacing at Readville (Boston), Mass., on Aug. 28, 1897, he became the first harness horse to go a mile in less than two minutes. His time was 1:59 1/4; his first trainer was the famed Edward F. Geers.

TENNESSEE HISTORICAL COMMISSION
Location: U.S. Highway 31, Spring Hill

HOOD'S RETREAT

Dec. 17, 1864. Moving rapidly south through Franklin, Stephen D. Lee's Corps with Chalmer's Cavalry Division attached, took up a delaying position in this area about 1:00 P.M. They beat off attacks by Wood's IV Corps & Wilson' Cavalry. Here Gen. Lee was wounded; command passed to Maj. Gen. Carter L. Stevenson. The Army of Tennessee bivouacked that night around Spring Hill.

TENNESSEE HISTORICAL COMMISSION
Location: U.S. Highway 31, Thompson's Station

The Battle of Franklin

Statue of Forrest on Roderick

THE BATTLE OF THOMPSON'S STATION

March 5, 1863. In the spring of 1863 the Federal Army operating out of Nashville made several foraging expeditions into this area collecting food and hay. At this site, General Earl Van Dorn's Confederate Cavalry Corps defeated a Federal task force under Col. John Coburn; he along with 1220 officers and men were captured. The outcome was decided by Forrest's Brigade which overran the Federal left several hundred yards northeast in a flank attack. In this action Forrest's famous horse "Roderick" was killed.

TENNESSEE HISTORICAL COMMISSION
Location: U.S. Highway 31, Thompson's Station

HOOD AND SCHOFIELD NOVEMBER 29, 1864

About 1/2 mile east, Buford's Division of Forrest's Cavalry Corps drove in pickets from Opdyke's and Lane's Federal Brigades and contained their defenses, extending west to the railroad. Meanwhile Stewart's Corps, marching north further eastward, with orders to bar the Nashville road, was halted by order from Hood. This caused the entire operation plan to fail, resulting in the Battles of Franklin and Nashville.

TENNESSEE HISTORICAL COMMISSION
Location: U.S. Highway 31, Thompson's Station

Historical Markers of Williamson County

Home to Giddens, Thompson, and Darby families

HOMESTEAD MANOR

Built between 1809 and 1819 by Francis Giddens, Revolutionary War gunsmith from Virginia, this house served as a refuge for neighbors during the Battle of Thompson's Station in 1863. During the fight, 17 year-old Alice Thompson, daughter of Dr. and Mrs. Elijah Thompson, dashed out of the cellar when she saw the color-bearer of the 3rd Arkansas Regiment fall. She retrieved his colors and inspired the regiment to carry the field. The house, which also served as a hospital during the battle, was listed on the National Register of Historic Places in 1977.

WILLIAMSON COUNTY HISTORICAL SOCIETY, 1991
Location: U.S. Highway 31, Thompson's Station

Thompson's Station Train Depot, circa 1910

THOMPSON'S STATION TRAIN DEPOT

Originally built 1866

This replica of the original depot was built in 1993 with monetary donations as well as donations of materials and labor from many different organizations and individuals. Materials were selected to comply as nearly as possible with the original structure.

The depot was called Thompson's Station in honor of Dr. Elijah Thompson who donated the land on which the village was built. Farmers drove their animals and products down the gravel roads to this depot for shipment to far away markets. Thompson's Station was known as the German Millet Capital of the World because of the large amount of the grain grown in the area.

There was a depot here before the one built in 1866. It is mentioned in a description of the Battle of Thompson's Station in an issue of the *Tennessee Historical Quarterly*. Apparently that one was destroyed in the battle and the other one built in 1866.

Location: Village of Thompson's Station

Burwood School, circa 1916

BURWOOD

Originally named Williamsburg, later Shaw, the village's name was changed to Burwood, a title taken from Mrs. Humphrey Ward's novel, "Robert Elsmere." Rev. John Pope, a Revolutionary War veteran, built his home, Eastview, here in 1806. Other early settlers included Samuel Akin, Bird Dodson, Fielding Helm, Elcain Johnson, Col. Hardy Murfree, Peter Parham, and Kinchen Sparkman. From 1826 until 1890, Cayce Springs Resort was renowned for its sulphur and mineral waters. The health spa included a hotel and guest cabins. Burwood School served the area from 1912 until 1976. Earlier, Williams Academy, established in 1879, was located in the village. Other schools, now gone, included West End, Sycamore, Pearly Hill, and Mt. LaVergene.

In 1818 "Parson" John Pope gave two acres, two miles south, for Pope's Chapel Methodist Church. After a 1910 cyclone destroyed the brick chapel, the congregation built, in 1913, the present Burwood Methodist Church. Burwood Church of Christ, originally known as West End, was moved to its present location in 1913. Lawrence Grove Baptist Church, located on the old Pope Campgrounds, was organized in 1917. Huff's Store, built in 1910, was placed on the National Register of Historic Places in 1988. Carter's Creek Pike, a toll road from 1850 until 1917, connects the area to Franklin.

BURWOOD COMMUNITY CLUB
WILLIAMSON COUNTY HISTORICAL SOCIETY, 1999
Location: Carter's Creek Pike, Burwood

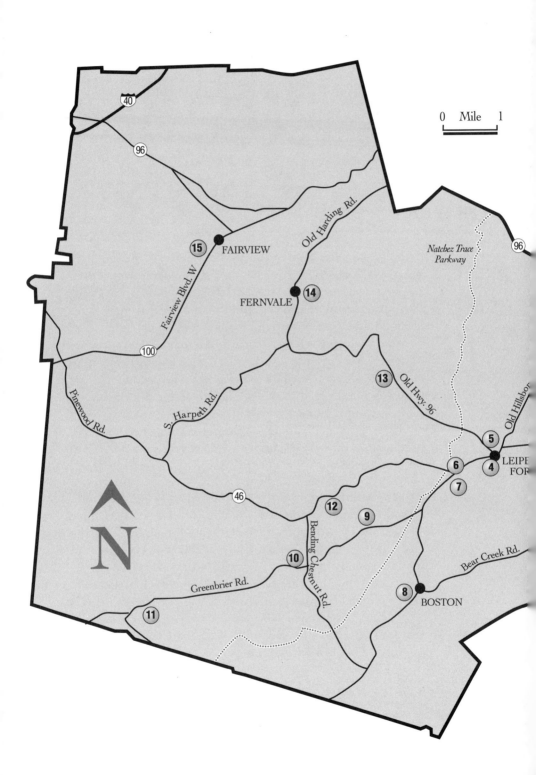

0　Mile　1

⑮ FAIRVIEW

Old Harding Rd.

Natchez Trace
Parkway

⑭ FERNVALE

Fairview Blvd. W

⑬ Old Hwy. 96

Old Hillsbor

Pinewood Rd.

S. Harpeth Rd.

⑤

⑥ LEIPE
FOR
④

⑦

⑫

⑨

Bending Chestnut Rd.

Bear Creek Rd.

⑩

Greenbrier Rd.

⑧ BOSTON

⑪

Part V

WESTERN
WILLIAMSON
COUNTY

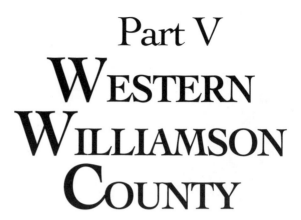

1 – Forest Hill
2 – Edward Swanson
3 – Southall
4 – Leiper's Fork Church of Christ
5 – Leiper's Fork
6 – Thomas Hart Benton
7 – Benton's Well and Slave Cabin
8 – Boston

9 – Garrison
10 – Bending Chestnut
11 – Greenbrier
12 – Richard "Dick" Poynor
13 – Kingfield
14 – Fernvale
15 – Evangeline Bowie, M.D.
16 – Bingham

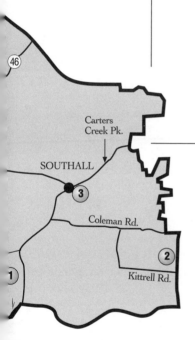

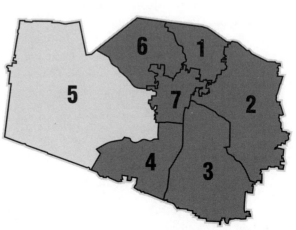

*Forest Hill School (above) and
T. F. Overbey home, circa 1914 (right)*

FOREST HILL

This community was named for the plantation of Thomas F. Perkins, originally a 1786 land grant of 640 acres to Hugh Leiper. This plantation, along with part of Col. Hardy Murfree's 5,000 acre tract, the farms of C. H. Kinnard, H. G. W. Mayberry, and S. S. Morton, and the smaller homesteads on Murfree's Fork, Bear Creek, and Carter's Creek Pike, constituted the community. In 1907 T. F. Overbey bought Forest Hill and, in 1914, built this handsome colonial revival home. Forest Hill Female Academy (1853–1949) became a public school after the Civil War. Area churches include Leiper's Fork and Murfree's Fork Primitive Baptist Churches, est. in 1824 and 1897. Glen Overbey operated a general store from 1916 until his death in 1973.

WILLIAMSON COUNTY HISTORICAL SOCIETY, 1999
Location: Carter's Creek Pike between Bear Creek and
West Harpeth Roads

EDWARD SWANSON (1759–1840)

Edward Swanson laid the foundation for a cabin one mile west prior to March 1780. This was the earliest known attempted white settlement in Williamson County. Swanson was one of eight men who came to the French Lick with James Robertson early in 1779 to plant corn in preparation for the settlement of what would later become Nashville. Marauding Indians made it impossible for Swanson to finish his homesteading effort, and he escaped to the safety of Fort Nashborough. Swanson barely missed death in hand-to-hand fighting with an Indian during the 1781 Battle of the Bluff. By 1800, he was living here where he eventually owned more than 1,000 acres. He is buried in the family cemetery near the homesite.

WILLIAMSON COUNTY HISTORICAL SOCIETY, 1997
Location: U.S. Highway 31 and Kittrell Road

Edward Swanson's home, destroyed by fire in 1967

Carbsil Plant at Southall

SOUTHALL

This community was named for James Southall, a soldier in the Battle of New Orleans. In 1876 Sam Allen, James Banks, J. S. Cotton, C. D. Kirkpatrick, Byron Lillie, and Theo Scruggs organized and built the Berea Church of Christ. A public school was located north of the church until 1953. White's Chapel Methodist Church, also organized in 1876, met until 1928. A post office was here from 1881 until 1904. The Carbsil Plant, operated by W. A. Johnson, processed paint pigment from locally mined shale from 1932 until 1947. Familiar community names include Alexander, Beard, Caldwell, Cannon, Coleman, Davis, Haffner, Haines, Hughes, Lane, McMillan, Mangrum, Nevils, Ormes, Sawyer, Vaughn, Whitley, and Yates.

WILLIAMSON COUNTY HISTORICAL SOCIETY, 1999
Location: Carter's Creek Pike, Southall

LEIPER'S FORK
CHURCH OF CHRIST

The Union Meeting House was built on this site in 1821. With the Restoration Movement and the preaching of Andrew Craig and Joel Anderson, Leiper's Fork became the first Church of Christ south of Nashville. In 1831, Seth and Rebecca Sparkman were the first members to be baptized for the remission of sins. David Lipscomb led a convention of Christians, who met here in 1862, to adopt positions as non-combatants in the Civil War. Their petition to Military Governor Andrew Johnson was rejected.

Leiper's Fork sponsored the Boston Church in 1854 and the Berea Church at Southall in 1876. The present building was built in 1877.

WILLIAMSON COUNTY HISTORICAL SOCIETY
Location: Highway 46, Village of Leiper's Fork

Leiper's Fork Church of Christ, first Church of Christ in Williamson County

*A. C. Lehew's store (top), Southall Bros. sawmill (inset), and
J. L. Sweeney's wagon factory (bottom)*

Leiper's Fork Bank building

LEIPER'S FORK

Situated on the Natchez Trace, the village and stream were named for pioneer surveyor Hugh Leiper. The Adams, Benton, Bond, Carl, Cummins, Davis, Dobbins, Hunter, Meadows, Parham, Southall, and Wilkins families were early settlers. Later the Sweeney, Inman, Locke, Lunn, Mayberry, Martin, Jones, and Burdette families lived here. Leiper's Fork had a post office from 1818 until 1918, a bank from 1912 until 1932, and a station on the 41.5 mile-long Middle Tennessee Railroad from 1910 until 1927. Hillsboro Academy (1890–1904), established by Professor Will Anderson, became a public school in 1905.

WILLIAMSON COUNTY HISTORICAL SOCIETY, 1996
Location: Old Hillsboro Road, Leiper's Fork

Portrait of Thomas Hart Benton, U.S. senator

THOMAS HART BENTON

On the foundation of this house was home of Thomas Hart Benton, whose family came from North Carolina in 1799. In 1809 he was state senator. Moving to Missouri in 1815, he became U.S. Senator in 1821, and remained in the senate 30 years. Dying at the age of 76, in 1858, he left a record of outstanding statesmanship.

TENNESSEE HISTORICAL COMMISSION
Location: Highway 46, Leiper's Fork
Corrections: The house referred to burned in 1982.
It is believed the Benton family did not come to the area until 1801.

Early slave log cabin (above) and Natchez Trace well (left)

BENTON'S WELL AND SLAVE CABIN

This seven-foot deep, hand-dug well and the slave cabin 115 yards south were once part of the 2,560 acre plantation of the Ann Gooch Benton family who moved here in 1801 from Hillsborough, N.C. The Benton home stood on the Natchez Road (now Old Hillsboro Road) slightly north of this cross-road.

In 1900, Will Martin's grist mill, granary, blacksmith shop and general store stood at the northwest corner of Old Hillsboro and Bailey Roads. In 1916, R. H. Pigue built the present building on the northeast corner. In 1929, Herman Green relocated his grocery there after a fire destroyed Martin's store where his store had been.

WILLIAMSON COUNTY HISTORICAL SOCIETY, 1995
Location: Intersection of Highway 46 and Bailey Road

Boston School (above) and Elder Seth and Rebecca Sparkman (inset)

BOSTON

In 1801, Revolutionary soldier William Sparkman settled on 320 acres on the headwaters of Leiper's Fork near the Duck River Ridge. In time, the Beasley, Davis, Marlin, Robinson, Skelley, Sudberry and Walls families became his neighbors. Later, the Carlisle, Denton, Hargrove, Hassell, King, McKee, Mealer, Shaw, Warf and Wilkes families moved to the community, which took the name Boston. The Boston Church of Christ, built in 1854 on land donated by Elder Seth Sparkman, became a leading force in the Restoration Movement. Boston School, established in 1858, remained until 1956. From 1850 until 1936, Boston had a post office.

WILLIAMSON COUNTY HISTORICAL SOCIETY, 1996
Location: Leiper's Creek Road at Sparkman Cemetery

Historical Markers of Williamson County

The Joe Jones home after the 1909 storm

GARRISON

In 1801, a U.S. Military garrison, under the command of Capt. Robert Butler, was established here to enforce the 1785 Indian boundary along the Duck River Ridge section of the new Natchez Trace. The Anderson, Burns, Campbell, Cowan, Cunningham, Harbison, Meacham, Peach, Poynor, Thweatt, and Wilkins families were among the first settlers. Garrison Methodist Church was organized in 1851 by Rev. Carroll C. Mayhew at Barr's Schoolhouse. Garrison School served the community from 1880 until 1945. The community was struck by a devastating cyclone on April 29, 1909, which killed eight people and destroyed much timber.

WILLIAMSON COUNTY HISTORICAL SOCIETY, 1996
Location: Garrison Road at Peach Hollow

BENDING CHESTNUT

The Indian practice of bending a chestnut sapling to the ground for marking trails gave this community its name. Such a tree stood at the crossroads which links Garrison to Greenbrier and Flagpole to Smarden. Fox's Store, established by T.C. and Jewel Fox in 1921, and Bending Chestnut School, which closed in 1954, are landmarks. Gilbert and T.C. Fox Jr. started Fox Brothers Sawmill in 1953, becoming the major employer in the community. Before Holt's Chapel Church of Christ and Bending Chestnut Baptist Church were organized, brush arbor meetings were popular religious events. Traditional area surnames include Anderson, Anglin, Beard, Burns, Edwards, Fox, Holt, McCandless, Rainey, Roberts, Swanson, Stinson, Tyner, and Whidby.

WILLIAMSON COUNTY HISTORICAL SOCIETY, 1999
Location: Crossroads of Garrison, Greenbrier, and Bending Chestnut Roads

Bending Chestnut School, closed in 1954

Greenbrier School

GREENBRIER

Revolutionary War soldiers John Beard, Henry W. Davis, John Mayberry, James Potts, and Thomas Prowell established homesteads and reared large families on Lick Creek. By 1811 Hugh Fox, Sampson Prowell and James Thompson had migrated from Burke County, N.C. Other early families to settle here were Beasley, Church, Edwards, Harris, Hay, Parham, Sears, Wakefield, and Warf. By 1831 regular Methodist camp meetings were held nearby. On April 29, 1909 the church, a school, Thompson's store, and much timber were destroyed by a cyclone. The present church was built in 1924 and the school, which closed in 1954, was built in 1929. White Oak Post Office served the area from 1876 until 1907.

DONATED BY THE GREENBRIER COMMUNITY
WILLIAMSON COUNTY HISTORICAL SOCIETY, 1998
Location: Greenbrier Road near Greenbrier Methodist Church
Correction: Rev. soldier Henry Mayberry in place of John Mayberry.

RICHARD "DICK" POYNOR

(1802–1882)

One of Tennessee's most outstanding wood craftsmen, Richard "Dick" Poynor was listed in the 1860 census as a free mulatto. He was literate, a man of property, and a member of the Leiper's Fork Primitive Church, a white congregation. Poynor's horse-powered lathe turned maple and hickory to create chairs and other items prized for their beauty and durability.

TENNESSEE HISTORICAL COMMISSION
Location: Pinewood Road

Enduring county treasures by Dick Poynor

Local woodcutters (left to right) Wm. "Buck" Howell, Houston King, Bob King,
Joe Hargrove, Elam Howell

KINGFIELD

In 1846, David and Sarah Hawks King came from Warren County, N.C. to settle fifty acres on Backbone Ridge between Leiper's Fork and Smith's Spring. Their homestead clearing among the vast forest gave Kingfield its name. The Kings reared a large family consisting of Katharine, Mary Ann, Peter, Madison, Clinton, Lorenzo, Washington, Richard, Solomon, and Sarah. Other Kingfield families include the descendants of William and Lafayette Howell, Bennett Hargrove, Nicholas Waller, David Furlough, John Burdette, and Stephen Wilson. The children of Kingfield attended Pond School from 1900 until 1949. Area churches include Pond Church of Christ and Kingfield Seventh-day Adventist, begun as a mission in 1917 and organized as a church in 1938.

WILLIAMSON COUNTY HISTORICAL SOCIETY, 1998
Location: Hargrove Road at David King Cemetery

FERNVALE

In 1822, Samuel Smith settled along the South Harpeth and soon the healing powers of the sulphur springs became well known. In 1879, John B. McEwen purchased Smith's Springs, renamed it Fernvale, and developed a popular summer resort with 114 guest hotel, Rialto, 10 acre park, icehouse, bathhouse, store, and post office. In 1904, railroad executive William Pepper Bruce bought the resort with 3,500 acres and continued operation of the hotel until it burned in 1910. Fernvale Methodist Church, organized in 1849, was built in 1885. Historic families include Allen, Givens, Harrison, Hughes, Inman, Ivy, King, Kirby, Page, Pewitt, and Sullivan. Area schools were Bedford, Cherokee, Coldwater, Forest Glen and Fernvale.

WILLIAMSON COUNTY HISTORICAL SOCIETY, 1999
Location: Old Harding Road

Fernvale Hotel (top) and Methodist Church (bottom)

Historical Markers of Williamson County

Evangeline Bowie, a woman of vision with a love for nature

EVANGELINE BOWIE, M.D. (1898–1992)

With her innovative ecology practices, Dr. Evangeline Bowie transformed this area from a washed-out, barren wasteland into a rich woodland and passed it along to her neighbors in Fairview. With the help of the financial acumen of her sister, Anna Bowie, M.D., and the nature love of her sister, Thelma Byrd Bowie, "Ms. Van" directed the reclaiming of the land and the planting of the trees to show the world what could be done to bring the earth back to its rightful heritage. This large acreage nature park is her legacy to generations of the future.

WILLIAMSON COUNTY HISTORICAL SOCIETY, 1997
Location: Bowie Nature Park, Fairview

Front view of Boyd's Mill (inset) and John Echels Boyd's farm, circa 1895 (above)

Historical Markers of Williamson County

Bingham bridge (above) and back view of Boyd's Mill (inset)

BINGHAM

Among the early landowners in this once-flourishing community on Old Hillsboro Road were members of the Boyd, Carter,
Haley, Hughes, Poynor, Reynolds, Short, and Stone families.
Bingham boasted Boyd's Mill on the West Harpeth, a federally
licensed distillery on Stillhouse Hollow Road, Lehew's saw
mill, Hog Eye Church, Charley Gray's and McMillan stores,
Blankenship's blacksmith shop, Bingham School, and a post
office from 1884 until 1907. The boyhood home of Matthew
Fontaine Maury, Pathfinder of the Seas, was located one mile
to the southeast. From 1843 until 1933, the County Poorhouse
was located one mile west.

WILLIAMSON COUNTY HISTORICAL SOCIETY, 1997
Location: Old Hillsboro Road and Boyd's Mill Pike

Part VI

NORTHERN WILLIAMSON COUNTY

1 – Forest Home
2 – Meeting of the Waters
3 – Old Natchez Trace Road
4 – Montpier
5 – Old Town
6 – Ash Grove
7 – Motheral/Moran House
8 – Grassland Community
9 – Beechville
10 – Harpeth Church

Natchez Trace Parkway

96

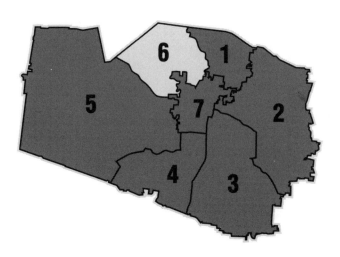

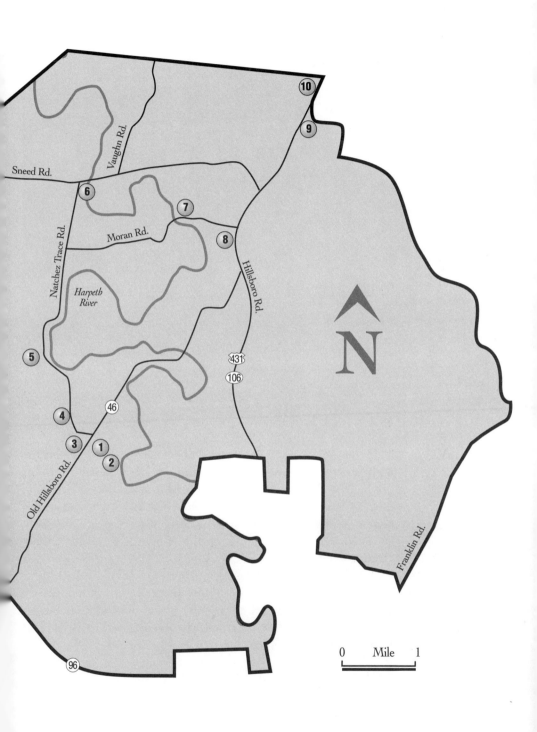

Sneed Rd.

Vaughn Rd.

Natchez Trace Rd.

Moran Rd.

Harpeth
River

Hillsboro Rd.

Old Hillsboro Rd.

Franklin Rd.

10

9

6

7

8

5

46

4

3

1

2

431

106

96

N

0   Mile   1

Miss Jane Bowman Owen's class, Forest Home School, circa 1910

FOREST HOME

This community, which appeared on an early twentieth century map "Forrest Home," is thought to have been named for Gen. Nathan B. Forrest, C.S.A. who found it a safe haven after his raid on Brentwood in March, 1863. Forest Home is near the center of what once were vast Perkins family plantations which included Hillside, Meeting of the Waters, Montpier, River Grange, Two Rivers, and Walnut Hill. For many years, two general stores faced each other at this intersection. McPherson's store was the voting place for the 6th District. The nearby Perkins School for the black children and Forest Home School for the white children were closed in 1949. The Forest Home Church of Christ was organized in 1950.

WILLIAMSON COUNTY HISTORICAL SOCIETY, 1997
Location: Old Hillsboro Road

Historical Markers of Williamson County

Meeting of the Waters, home to Perkinses since early 1800s

MEETING OF THE WATERS

This house, named for its location at the confluence of the Big Harpeth and West Harpeth Rivers, was built in the early 1800s by Thomas Harden Perkins (1757–1838), Revolutionary War officer, Tennessee pioneer, planter, and ironmaster. It is one of the five notable Perkins houses still standing in Williamson County. Inherited in 1838 by Perkins's daughter Mary and her husband, Nicholas "Bigbee" Perkins of Montpier, it passed to their son Nicholas Edwin in 1848.

WILLIAMSON COUNTY HISTORICAL SOCIETY, 1990
Location: 3200 Del Rio Pike

Modern Natchez Trace expansion bridge over Highway 96 West

OLD NATCHEZ TRACE ROAD

This stone is erected to preserve the memory of the Natchez Trace Road, which ran a short distance westward from this point and converged to the line of this pike following its general course. It continued southwest to Cunningham's Bridge and up the hill to Duck River Ridge where it joined the Trace (Proper) end to end. The Natchez Trace was opened under treaties with Chickasaws and Choctaws made in 1801. It was for many years the great highway from Natchez to Nashville.

ERECTED BY TENNESSEE D.A.R. APRIL 11, 1912
Location: Old Hillsboro Road at Forest Home

Montpier today (above), built by Nicholas Perkins (inset)

MONTPIER

Nicholas "Bigbee" Perkins (1779–1848) gained national fame when he helped capture Aaron Burr in the Mississippi Territory in 1807. Perkins, who was a lawyer and territorial Register of Lands, also was in charge of a small party who took Burr from Ft. Stoddart to Richmond, Virginia where Burr was tried and acquitted of treason. After returning to Tennessee, Perkins acquired about 12,000 acres in this area and, in 1821–22, built Montpier, where he lived until 1838 when he and his wife Mary moved to Meeting of the Waters approximately one mile to the southeast.

WILLIAMSON COUNTY HISTORICAL SOCIETY, 1991
Location: Old Natchez Trace near Forest Home

OLD TOWN

The highly developed Indian society which flourished here between 900 and 1450 A.D. is now marked by several earth mounds in the field south of this marker. The village was surrounded by a palisade wall. Nearby are dry laid stone abutments of a bridge built over Brown Creek (formerly Donelson Creek) by the U.S. Government in 1801 to facilitate travel on the Natchez Trace. The house 300 yards south, was built by Thomas Brown ca. 1854. It and the bridge were placed on the National Register of Historic Places in 1988, the Indian site in 1989.

WILLIAMSON COUNTY HISTORICAL SOCIETY, 1991
Location: Old Natchez Trace

Stone bridge abutment over Brown's Creek (top) and Thomas Brown's 1854 home (bottom)

The covered Union Bridge and Squire J. S. Stockett's car

ASH GROVE

Ash Grove community in Sawyer's Bend of the Harpeth River was known for its Union Bridge, built jointly by Davidson and Williamson Counties. Burned during the Civil War, the bridge was replaced in 1881. Before being washed away in the flood of 1948, it was the last covered bridge on the Harpeth. The Armstrong, Cator, Davis, Hill, Hulme, Moran, Morris, Pearre, Phipps, Sawyer, Stockett, and Vaughan families were prominent here. Ash Grove Cumberland Presbyterian Church was built in 1893 on land donated by Dempsey R. Sawyer. With its closing in 1967, and the earlier closing of the public school in 1946, the community lost most of its identity.

WILLIAMSON COUNTY HISTORICAL SOCIETY, 1996
Location: Old Natchez Trace near Sneed Road

Motheral/Moran House overlooks the Harpeth River

MOTHERAL/MORAN HOUSE

This house was built before 1815 by John Motheral (1755–1824), a Revolutionary War soldier. Originally, the large log home faced the Harpeth River. When the road was moved, a double front porch was added on the north side, the logs were covered over, and a frame addition built. In 1873, Motheral heirs sold the farm to Nathan and Margaret Linton Greer. After Mr. Greer's death, his widow and second wife, Harriet Elizabeth Henry Greer, a collateral descendant of Patrick Henry, married, in 1890, Edward Hicks Moran, a magistrate for 34 years. They lived here as did their only son, Sam Henry Moran (1894–1955), and his family. Sam Moran served 17 years as a magistrate and three terms in the state legislature.

WILLIAMSON COUNTY HISTORICAL SOCIETY, 1997
Location: Moran Road near the Harpeth River Bridge

Red Cross Grassland Volunteers, 1918 (above) and the Jeff Moran home (inset)

GRASSLAND COMMUNITY

This site was part of a 1784 land grant to heirs of Wm. Leaton Jr. The tract was settled in the late 1820s by Wm. Leaton III. By 1801, John Campbell, John Stuart, Ephraim Brown, Wm. Tarkington, and Joseph German were living in this area. Later, Grassland families were Leigh, Motheral, Fullton, Sneed, Murrey, Armstrong, Hulme, Greer, Moran, Wray, and Hughes. In 1846, Prior Smith bought the Leaton farm and enlarged the two-room log cabin, the district's first voting place, to a ten-room house known as the Jeff Moran home. The community had blacksmith shops, country stores, a post office (1876–1902), and Grassland School. Bethlehem United Methodist Church was organized in 1848.

WILLIAMSON COUNTY HISTORICAL SOCIETY, 1997
Location: Hillsboro Road at River Rest

BEECHVILLE

Samuel McCutchen, Charles Brown, and Samuel Edmiston settled here before 1800. Thomas W. Stockett, who built a mill on Little Harpeth River, came by 1802. Near the intersection of Beech Creek Road and the Nashville-Hillsboro Turnpike were various businesses—saddletree and wagon makers, a blacksmith shop, saw mill, two stores, post office (1876–1903), and a tool gate. A Masonic lodge and Harpeth Academy shared a building north of Harpeth Presbyterian Church. Community schools were Oak Hill, Sunnyside, and Beechville (black). Doctors M.T. Byrn, W.J. Parker and John Sugg attended the area's medical needs. Greater Pleasant View Baptist Church, organized in 1894, moved from Sneed Road to Hillsboro ca. 1932.

THE FAMILY OF BATTLE AND SARA PURYEAR RODES
WILLIAMSON COUNTY HISTORICAL SOCIETY, 1997
Location: Hillsboro Road south of Beech Creek Road

Beechville School

Harpeth Church, typical two-front-door, brick church of the early nineteenth century

HARPETH CHURCH

This church is built on ground donated by Samuel McCutchen, a Revolutionary War veteran who received it as part of a land grant. O. B. Hayes served as the first pastor; David Bell and Robert McCutchen were elders, and James McCutchen was secretary. The church was housed in a log building from 1811 until 1836 when work on the present building began.

TENNESSEE HISTORICAL COMMISSION
Location: Hillsboro Road on the Davidson County line

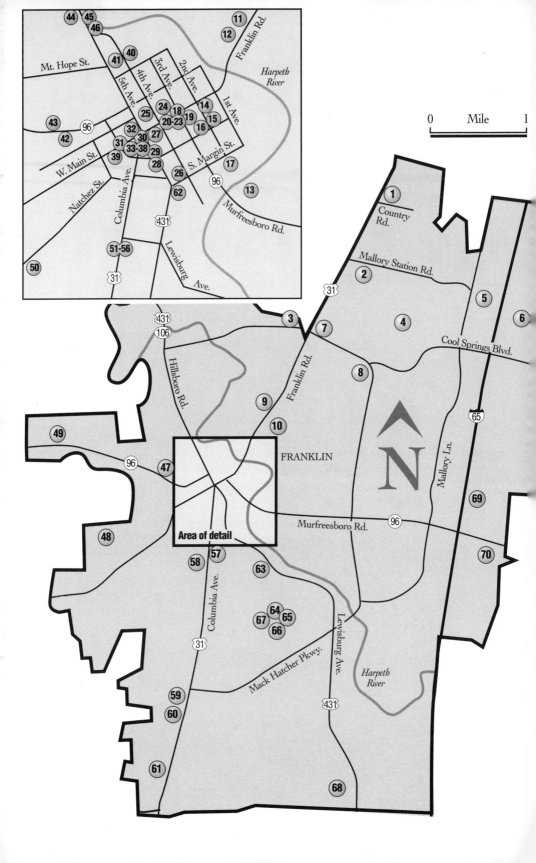

Part VII FRANKLIN

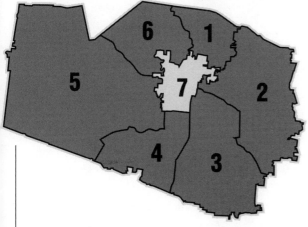

HOME DEMONSTRATION CLUBS

Ida Allen McKay 1848–1927. President of first Home Demonstration Club in Tennessee.

ERECTED IN HER MEMORY BY PIONEER H.D. CLUB
Location: U.S. Highway 31 at Highgate Drive, Franklin

Early Home Demonstration Club organizer Virginia Carson (top) and the Hillsboro Home Demonstration Club (bottom), organized in 1928, one of the oldest active clubs in Williamson County

Franklin Interurban trains carried passengers from Franklin Square to Nashville Square hourly

FRANKLIN INTERURBAN

In 1902, eight Nashville businessmen (Frank Bond, James Fulcher, Frank Haskell, John H. McMillen, James L. Parkes Jr., Charles Ruth, W. H. Whittemore, and D. J. Wikle) formed the Nashville and Columbia Railroad. Completed in 1908, the Interurban was an electric train, which ran from Franklin, where it circled the town square, to Nashville. The cars ran from 7 a.m. until 11:30 p.m. and carried both passengers and freight. Henry Hunter Mayberry, who raised money for the venture and who became president in 1905, was instrumental in its success. The Interurban converted to gasoline powered buses in 1942, a year after the Nashville Coach Company did so. The Interurban ceased operations in 1969.

WILLIAMSON COUNTY HISTORICAL SOCIETY, 1999
Location: Mallory Road off Nashville Pike, Franklin

GLEN ECHO

This classic two-story Federal-style house was built ca 1829 by Judge Thomas Stuart, Williamson County's first Circuit Judge. It features Flemish Bond brickwork on the front and American Bond on the sides and rear. The "glorified pioneer" floor plan, common to Middle Tennessee, remains unaltered. The interior contains a large amount of original woodwork, including built-in cabinets in each room. During the Civil War, Confederate and Federal soldiers camped on the grounds. In 1862, General Don Carlos Buell's Federal Army could be seen from the back porch as it marched to Shiloh. In 1996, Glen Echo became a focal point of Battle Ground Academy's new Upper School campus. The house was completely renovated and restored in 1998.

WILLIAMSON COUNTY HISTORICAL SOCIETY, 1999
Location: BGA North campus, Franklin

Recent drawing of Glen Echo, which centers the new BGA campus

McEwen Cemetery, resting place of Williamson County pioneers

McEwen Cemetery

David McEwen, one of the first settlers to come to this area in 1798, set aside this plot as his family's burying ground. David and Margaret Ervin McEwen and four generations of their descendants are buried here. Included are three sons and their spouses, James and Elizabeth Goff McEwen; Christopher Ervin McEwen and his two wives, Rebecca Brown McEwen and Narcissa Newsom McEwen; and John Lapsey and Tabitha H. Barfield McEwen. Two daughters, Jane McEwen and Eleanor Caroline McEwen Stevens, and David's pioneer brother, William McEwen, are also buried here. The McEwens, a large and influential family, were prominent in Williamson County for many decades after its 1799 inception.

WILLIAMSON COUNTY HISTORICAL SOCIETY, 1999
Location: Wyndchase Apartments, Aspen Grove Parkway, Franklin

MALLORY SPRINGHOUSE

Long before Thomas Sharp Spencer was granted the surrounding 320 acres in 1788 for his Revolutionary War service, Native Americans used this spring as a camp site. Numerous stone artifacts found nearby attest to their presence. The springhouse dates to John and Sarah Crockett Mallory, who purchased 105 acres from Elizabeth Spencer in 1813. In modern times, the spring supplied water for the Pratt Dairy, four family households, and Mallory School. Students carried buckets of water to refresh their classmates until the school closed in 1949. This early 19th century springhouse, today situated within a thriving commerce center, symbolizes the enormous transformation Williamson County has experienced in two centuries.

IN MEMORY OF MARVIN H. PRATT SR.
BY HIS WIFE, ESTER, AND CHILDREN
HERITAGE FOUNDATION
OF WILLIAMSON COUNTY AND FRANKLIN, 1999
Location: Mallory Lane near Cool Springs Galleria, Franklin

Mallory Springhouse

Robert Blake Carothers

CAROTHERS FAMILY

Robert Carothers Sr., a Revolutionary War soldier, and his family came to Tennessee from North Carolina in 1791 and were living in Williamson County in 1799. His son, James, a War of 1812 veteran, became a prosperous landowner well-known for his nearby Pleasant Exchange Plantation. Robert Carothers Jr. and his family owned land adjacent to this marker. James' son, Thomas Jefferson Carothers, was a Confederate soldier. James sold his two-story log house to another son, Robert Blake Carothers, who enlarged it. Owned by the Carothers family almost fifty years, this historic Cool Springs House was moved in 1993 from Franklin to Crockett Park in Brentwood.

COOL SPRINGS REAL ESTATE ASSOCIATES
WILLIAMSON COUNTY HISTORICAL SOCIETY, 1998
Location: Cool Springs Boulevard near the Convention Center, Franklin

FIRST PRESBYTERIAN CHURCH

First Presbyterian Church was organized on June 8, 1811 with 46 members, including four newly ordained elders. The founding pastor, The Rev. Gideon Blackburn, was a noted preacher, teacher, founder of numerous churches, and schools, and a missionary to the Cherokees. The congregation built a meeting house adjacent to the City Cemetery in 1815. It relocated to the corner of Fifth Avenue and Main Street in 1842, where it remained for 152 years. On September 18, 1994, this building was dedicated to the Glory of God, continuing a history of Reformed worship, Christian education, and local and world mission.

Sola gratia. solo Christo. sola fide. sola scriptura.

WILLIAMSON COUNTY HISTORICAL SOCIETY, 1997
Location: U.S. Highway 31 and Legends Drive, Franklin

First Presbyterian Church (1842–1888)

Roper's Knob, Franklin's highest point

ROPER'S KNOB

The large hill immediately to the south, which rises more than 900 feet above sea level, played an important role in the Civil War. Used as a signal station by Union troops, Roper's Knob was a key communications link between Nashville and points south and between Franklin and Murfreesboro. After Middle Tennessee was occupied by Federal troops in early 1862, the hill was crowned with entrenchments and an octagonal log blockhouse. A sophisticated pulley system helped lift artillery to the summit. The knob, along with nearby Fort Granger, helped guard the Tennessee & Alabama Railroad. Roper's Knob was not occupied at the time of the Battle of Franklin, November 30, 1864.

WILLIAMSON COUNTY HISTORICAL SOCIETY, 1997
Location: Mack Hatcher Parkway at Cool Springs Boulevard, Franklin

MIDNIGHT SUN 410751
1940-1965

Midnight Sun

MIDNIGHT SUN
No. 410751

The Horse of the Century
1940–1965
The Champion under Saddle
The Champion as a Sire
The Champion of the Breed

Location: Harlinsdale Stables, U.S. Highway 31, Franklin

Historical Markers of Williamson County

Magic Chef factory occupied the Allen site 1955–1959

ALLEN MANUFACTURING COMPANY

This complex of ten depression-era buildings, with a total of 310,000 square feet, housed four different factories over its industrial lifetime. The buildings were built for the Allen Manufacturing Co. (stove manufacturers) in 1929. More than $100,000 worth of preferred stock was sold locally to finance their construction.

After Allen Manufacturing went in receivership during the Great Depression, the Dortch Stove Works (1932–1955), Magic Chef (1955–1959) and Jamison Bedding Works (1962–1991) successively occupied this site, where more than 300 people once worked. In 1997–98, the complex was renovated by Franklin businessman Calvin LeHew as a commercial, retail, and entertainment center.

WILLIAMSON COUNTY HISTORICAL SOCIETY, 1998
Location: U.S. Highway 31, Franklin

JOHN PRICE BUCHANAN

 Born 3 mi. NE Oct. 24, 1847. Member of the Legislature, 1887 to 1891, he was governor from 1891 to 1893. Elected by a farmer-labor coalition, his administration was marked by labor unrest and reform, extension of the public school system and granting of Confederate pensions. He died May 14, 1930, and is buried in Murfreesboro.

TENNESSEE HISTORICAL COMMISSION
Location: Riverside Drive and U.S. Highway 31, Franklin

John Price Buchanan, Tennessee's agrarian governor

Riverview (above), home of H. H. Mayberry, a man of vision (inset)

RIVERVIEW

Built in 1902 by Henry Hunter Mayberry (1861–1931) a native of Williamson County and a man of integrity, broad vision and generosity. He was a developer of Franklin's water system and gave the only spring large enough to service it. In 1908 he was the builder and president of the Franklin-Nashville Interurban, the first in the state. Its hourly service resulted in the town's increased business growth with Nashville. Mr. Mayberry also built the Nashville-Gallatin Interurban.

SPONSORED BY THE
WILLIAMSON COUNTY BICENTENNIAL COMMITTEE, 1976
Location: U.S. Highway 31, Franklin

Franklin

FORT GRANGER

In the spring of 1863, Federal forces commanded by Maj. Gen. Gordon Granger occupied Franklin. Construction of major fortifications began under the direction of Capt. W. E. Merrill, U.S. Corps of Engineers, the largest of them being placed on Figuers Bluff, .2 of a mile north of the Harpeth River. Fort Granger commanded the southern and northern approaches to Franklin and was adjacent to the critically important Tenn. & Ala. Railroad bridge. The artillery within the fort saw action twice in 1863 against Confederate cavalry forces. During the Battle of Franklin, Nov. 30, 1864, the site served as Hqtrs. of Maj. Gen. John M. Schofield (commander of U.S. forces) and as an active artillery position.

WILLIAMSON COUNTY HISTORICAL SOCIETY, 1989
Location: Pinkerton Park, Franklin

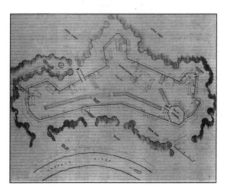

Drawings of Fort Granger (left) and
Franklin Battlefield (above), now City Park

Peggy O'Neale Eaton   *John H. Eaton*

JOHN H. EATON

On this site stood the home of John H. Eaton, U.S. Senate (1818–1829) and Secretary of War under Andrew Jackson (1829–1831). He resigned from the Cabinet after a scandal which reflected on the reputation of his controversial wife Peggy. He served as Governor of the Territory of Florida (1834–1836) and as Minister of Spain (1838–1840). Eaton retired from public life in 1840. He sold this property in 1843 and lived in Washington, D.C. until his death.

TENNESSEE HISTORICAL COMMISSION
Location: 125 East Main, Franklin

Masonic Temple, Franklin's architectural treasure

MASONIC TEMPLE

This Masonic Temple, home of Hiram Lodge No. 7, built in 1823, was the first three story building west of the Allegheny Mountains. It has been occupied by Hiram Lodge No. 7 since its completion, making it one of the oldest continuous Lodges at the same location in the United States. It was the site of President Andrew Jackson's Treaty with the Chickasaw Indians in 1830, and served as an observation post and hospital at the time of the Battle of Franklin in November, 1864.

WILLIAMSON COUNTY HISTORICAL SOCIETY, 1984
Location: Third Avenue South, Franklin

EWEN CAMERON

On this site in 1798 Ewen Cameron built the first house in the town of Franklin. Cameron was born Feb. 23, 1768 in Balgalkan, Ferintosh, Scotland. He emigrated to Virginia in 1785 and from there came to Tennessee. Cameron died Feb. 28, 1846, having lived forty-eighty years in the same log house. He and his second wife, Mary, are buried in the Old City Cemetery. His descendants have lived in Franklin continuously since 1798 when his son Duncan was the first white child born here.

WILLIAMSON COUNTY HISTORICAL SOCIETY, 1992
Location: Third Avenue South, Franklin

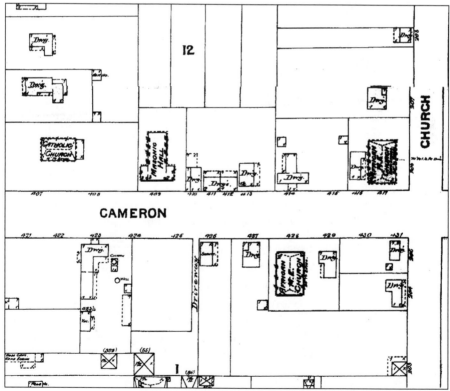

1893 Sanborn-Perris map of Cameron Street, now Second Avenue South

The Franklin Railroad passenger depot (above) and freight depot (inset)

FRANKLIN RAILROAD DEPOT

Belching smoke and whistle screaming at 7:30 A.M. on Tuesday, March 6, 1855, TENNESSEE & ALABAMA RR CO.'s first train pulled into this depot site. The second RR constructed in the State, it was soon completed to Thompson Station, later to Columbia, Pulaski, finally to Decatur, AL. The roadbed was seized by the Federal forces in 1862 but the rolling stock fell in the hands of the Confederates and vanished. Reorganized in 1866 as the Nashville and Decatur RR it was leased and then purchased by L & N RR. It has remained in continuous operation since then.

John C. Claybrook, a Williamson County RR visionary, led a group of about 30 local citizens in 1852 to provide the initial $20,000 capital. The City of Franklin followed with $20,000. Once the company had graded and prepared 20 miles of roadbed from Nashville with stone and cross ties, the State of Tennessee paid for the English-made iron rails by issuing 6% long bonds at the rate of $10,000 per mile.

WILLIAMSON COUNTY HISTORICAL SOCIETY, 1999
Location: South Margin Street, Franklin

Dedication Day, November 30, 1899

CONFEDERATE MONUMENT

37 feet 8 inches of Vermont granite shaft and 6 foot tall Carrar marble statue

Erected to Confederate Soldiers by Franklin Chapter No. 14, Daughters of the Confederacy

Nov. 30 A.D. 1899

"We who saw them and knew them well are witnesses to coming ages of their valor and fidelity; tried and true, glory crowned. 1861–1865"

"Would not it be a shame for us
If their memory past from our land and hearts,
And a wrong to them and a shame to us.
The glories they won shall not wane for us.
In legend and lay our Heroes in Grey
Shall ever live over again for us."

Location: Public Square, Franklin

DOWNTOWN FRANKLIN HISTORIC DISTRICT

The town of Franklin was developed in 1799 by Abram Maury who bought the land from Anthony Sharpe. The original town, consisting of 109 acres, was composed of sixteen blocks divided into 188 lots centered on a public square. The historic district, placed on the National Register of Historic Places in 1972, is outlined by Margin streets on the north and south and includes First, Second, Third, Fourth, and Fifth streets running north and south, and Church, Main, and Bridge streets running east and west. About 300 commercial and residential buildings lie within the district. A majority are from the 19th century with an additional fifty-two being constructed between 1907 and 1941. Franklin received its town charter in 1815.

HERITAGE FOUNDATION OF
FRANKLIN AND WILLIAMSON COUNTY
WILLIAMSON COUNTY HISTORICAL SOCIETY, 1999
Location: City Hall, Public Square, Franklin

Original town plat by Abram Maury

One of seven Tennessee antebellum courthouses,
Williamson County Courthouse was featured on an
early Franklin postcard (right)

COURTHOUSE

Williamson County's first courthouses, one log and one brick, were in the center of the square. This, the third, completed in 1858 under the supervision of John W. Miller, is one of seven antebellum courthouses in Tennessee. The four iron columns were smelted at Fernvale and cast at a Franklin foundry. It was used as a Federal headquarters during the Civil War and served as a hospital after the Battle of Franklin. The interior was remodeled in 1937, 1964, and 1976. The annex was added in 1976.

WILLIAMSON COUNTY HISTORICAL SOCIETY, 1976
Location: Courthouse Yard, Public Square, Franklin

REVOLUTIONARY WAR SOLDIERS

 This tablet is placed commemorative of the Revolutionary soldiers buried in Williamson County by Old Glory Chapter D.A.R. organized by Miss Susie Gentry 1887. John Allen, William Allen, John Andrews, Mark Andrews, Frederick C. Bass, John Beard, Anson Burk, Minos Cannon, Henry Cook, William Crutcher, Col. Guilford Dudley, John Echols, John Evans, Thornton Ferguson, Henry Garrett, Watson Gentry, Andrew Goff, Jacob Crimmer, Robert Cutwate, Laban Hartley, Samuel Henderson, Daniel Hill, Major Green Hill, George Hulme, John McAllister Hutton, William A. McCoy, Peter Leslie, Moses Lindsey, Rev. John Atkinson, Joshua Pearre, Col. William White, Col. Peter Perkins, Tarpley Lightfoot, William Lockridge, Samuel McCutcheon, Daniel McMahon, Robert Mallory, William Marshall, Col. William Martin, Col. Hardy Murfree, Nelson R. Nailling, George Neely, Robert Osborn, Lt. Hardin Perkins, Joseph Phillips, Miles Priest, Moses Priest, James Potts, James Ragsdale, Jacob Scott, John Secrest, Maj. Anthony Sharp, Henry Sledge, Sherrod Smith, David Squires, Edward Swanson, James Turner, Richard Vernon, Daniel White, Jason Wilson, William Redford, James Sheppard.

GIFT OF ANDREW CROCKETT
Location: On the face of the Courthouse, Franklin

Roll of Honor
World War I (1917–1919)

In memory of the soldiers of Williamson County who made the supreme sacrifice in the World's greatest struggle for freedom 1914–1918. "Greater lover hath no man than this, that a man lay down his life for his friends." E. B. Anderson, Jas. D. Anderson, Ed. M. Byrd, W. S. Caldwell, Jno. D. Carter, C. A. Chilson, Zack A. Green, M. E. Grigsby, W. E. Holt, Jas. W. Holt, M. C. Hassell, Cecil Hughes, Clifton Jones, Owen B. Layne, Wm. E. Logan, J. C. Lankford. Jas. W. Moran, F. C. McClannahan, Jas. L. McGee, J. W. Morgan, Tom W. Maddox, Floyd Reed, Frank M. Ring, J. E. Stephens, Otis Sharpe, Joe B. Warren, W. M. Marlin. Colored: Jas. Anderson, Solomon Davis, Richard Fly, Jas. T. Johnson, Jimmie King, W. N. Thomas.

PLACED BY
THE WILLIAMSON COUNTY ARMY COMFORT CIRCLE 1921
ORGANIZED APR. 20, 1917
Location: On the face of the Courthouse, Franklin

Law Enforcement Officers
Killed in Line of Duty

Sheriff M. H. Stephens, killed June 27, 1919. Constable Sam Locke, killed March 7, 1925. Constable Matt Sullivan, killed October 29, 1933. Constable Clarence W. Reed, killed January 28, 1944. Deputy Sheriff Morris Heithcock, killed June 28, 1972.

DEDICATED BY THE MORRIS HEITHCOCK LODGE NO 41
FRATERNAL ORDER OF POLICE
Location: Courthouse Yard, Franklin

MAURY-DARBY BUILDING

This oldest building on the Square was built 1815–1817 by Thomas T. Maury, cousin of Matthew Fontaine Maury, "Pathfinder of the Seas," and nephew of Abram Maury, Franklin's founder. It has housed Franklin's first bank, "doctors' shops," other business and law offices.

WILLIAMSON COUNTY HISTORICAL SOCIETY, 1991
Location: Public Square, Franklin

Maury-Darby Building (second building from left), oldest building on the Public Square

Fourth Avenue Church of Christ (1928–1978)

FOURTH AVENUE
CHURCH OF CHRIST

In 1833, a congregation of seventeen Christians was organized in Franklin following preaching by Tolbert Fanning, Absalom Adams, and Alexander Campbell. Joel Anderson and Andrew Craig were other early leaders in this church, one of the oldest in the American Restoration movement. After Campbell's second visit in 1851, a brick meeting house was erected here on Indigo Street on a lot given by Thomas Hardin Perkins. The first service was held September 5, 1852. That building, used as a hospital after the Battle of Franklin, stood until it was ruined by a cyclone in 1927. The second church, which featured stained-glass windows from a 1914 edition, stood here for fifty years. The present structure was built in 1978.

WILLIAMSON COUNTY HISTORICAL SOCIETY, 1996
Location: Fourth Avenue, North, Franklin

TENNESSEE FEMALE COLLEGE

1854–1886
1887–1916

Location: Fourth Avenue South, Franklin

Tennessee Female College, leading school for area females until 1916; first building (top) burned in 1886, second building (bottom) was torn down in 1916

Presbyterian Church (left) and the church in 1888 (above)

PRESBYTERIAN CHURCH

The Presbyterian Church was organized in Franklin by the Reverend Gideon Blackburn on June 8, 1811 and first located near the City Cemetery. The church moved to this location in 1842. The Reverend A. N. Cunningham was pastor from 1843 to 1857. In 1847, he founded the Franklin Female Institute, which was temporarily housed here. After the Battle of Franklin, the building was used as a hospital by Federal troops and severely damaged. In 1888, a house of worship in the Romanesque Revival style of H. H. Richardson was erected. After a fire in 1905, the church was rebuilt in 1908. In 1992, those members of the congregations who wished to remain on this historic site, organized the Historic Franklin Presbyterian Church.

WILLIAMSON COUNTY HISTORICAL SOCIETY, 1997
Location: Main Street and Fifth Avenue, South, Franklin

Franklin

Franklin's tallest spire shown on an early postcard (right) of the Methodist Church

METHODIST CHURCH

This building stands at the church's third location. The original brick sanctuary stood on the east side of First Avenue facing Church Street. Land for it had been given in 1799 by Franklin's founder Abram Maury. Pioneer Methodist Bishop Francis Asbury preached there in 1812. The church relocated in 1830 to the N.E. corner of Second and Church. That building was used as a hospital during the Battle of Franklin. Following the Civil War, the congregation of 238 purchased this triangular lot for $300. Construction began in 1869, with completion in 1871 and expansions in 1882, 1916, 1949, and 1955. The spire destroyed in 1927, was replaced in 1995.

WILLIAMSON COUNTY HISTORICAL SOCIETY, 1995
Location: Fifth Avenue South, Franklin

POST OFFICE

A.W. Mellon
Secretary of the Treasury
James A. Wetmore
Acting Supervisory Architect
1924

Location: Post Office at Five Points, Franklin

Five Points before 1924 (bottom) where the new post office (top) was built in 1929

CHICKASAW TREATY COUNCIL

In the spring of 1830 Congress passed the Indian Removal Act providing the President with the means to exchange the lands of the five civilized Indian nations of the Southeast for lands west of the Mississippi. On August 20, 1830 Andrew Jackson met in Franklin with the Chiefs of the Chickasaw nation to begin a series of treaties which removed the tribe to Oklahoma. "Sharpe Knife" as the chiefs called Jackson, was the only President ever to attend an Indian removal council.

TENNESSEE HISTORICAL SOCIETY
Location: Five Points, Franklin

President Jackson visited Franklin for treaty talks

Five Points looking west, featuring Franklin Cumberland Presbyterian Church on left

FRANKLIN CUMBERLAND PRESBYTERIAN CHURCH

Founded in 1871 as Franklin's First Cumberland Presbyterian Church, the cornerstone was laid in June 3, 1876. Designed by H. C. Thompson, architect of Nashville's Ryman Auditorium, the church was dedicated on April 16, 1877, with the Rev. Thomas Dale serving as first minister. This Gothic Revival church was listed on the National Register of Historic Places as part of the Hincheyville Historic District in 1982.

TENNESSEE HISTORICAL COMMISSION
Location: West Main Street, Franklin

Franklin

Present St. Paul's Episcopal Church (left) and in the 1930s (above)

ST. PAUL'S EPISCOPAL CHURCH

This "Mother Church of the Diocese of Tennessee" was begun in 1831, four years after its congregation was organized in 1827. Here James H. Otey, its first rector, was elected the first bishop of Tennessee. It was so damaged through use as a Civil War barracks and hospital that it had to be remodeled in 1870. It is the oldest Episcopal church and congregation in Tennessee, and the oldest Episcopal Church building in continual use west of the Appalachians.

TENNESSEE HISTORICAL COMMISSION
Location: West Main Street, Franklin

Historical Markers of Williamson County

Franklin mystery — "What became of the brass cannon?"

WAR OF 1812

On his return from New Orleans Andrew Jackson gave a brass cannon to Franklin. A part of his soldiery camped here on their way to New Orleans.

PLACED BY COL. THOS. HART BENTON
CHAPTER U.S.D. OF 1812 IN 1917
Location: Five Points, Franklin

Reverend Gideon Blackburn   *Bishop James Hervey Otey*

1911

This tablet commemorates Rev. Gideon Blackburn, D.D. and James Hervey Otey, D.D. LL. D. as early educators of Williamson Co. The first and second principals of Harpeth Academy from 1811 to 1827. Gideon Blackburn born in Va. Aug. 27, 1772, founded Presbyterianism in this Co. Jan. 14, 1811. Died in Carlinsville, Illinois Aug. 23, 1838. James Hervey Otey born in Va. Jan. 27, 1800. Founded the Episcopal Church in Tenn, Aug. 25, 1827. Consecrated first bishop of Tenn. Jan. 14, 1834. Died April 23, 1863.

PLACED BY OLD GLORY CHAPTER
DAUGHTERS OF THE AMERICAN REVOLUTION
Location: Williamson County Library entrance, Franklin

1910

This tablet is placed in honor and as a tribute to Com. Matthew Fountaine Maury. The Pathfinder of the Seas. Born Jan'y 14, 1806. Died Feb'y 1, 1873. Scientist, hydrographer, diplomat, U.S. and Confederate Naval officer. America's most distinguished citizen and Williamson County's adopted son.

PLACED BY OLD GLORY CHAPTER
DAUGHTERS OF THE AMERICAN REVOLUTION
Location: Williamson County Library entrance, Franklin

Commodore Matthew F. Maury

ROLL OF HONOR
WORLD WAR II (1941–1945)

Robert E. Akin
Donald C. Alexander
L. G. Allen Jr.
Roy F. Alley
Ernest Brown Barnes
James A. Beard
Wallace Booker
Bennie R. Bradley
William A. Broadwell
Curtis C. Brown
Eugene Lewis Brown
Charles Buchanan
Emory Buchanan
Scobey A. Burchett
Simon Burdette
Dewey Burns
Vance Burke
Robert Shannon Burke Jr.
Ralph D. Campbell
Silas McKay Carlisle
Roy Caruthers
Beverly Lofton Chadwell
John Overton Colton
James Robert Cothran
W. H. Culverson
Roy Davis
H. R. Dodson
H. R. Dobbs
Mark A. Dobbs
Jessie R. Dorris
Albertson D. Eley
Glenn Eley
Brooks Fleming Jr.
Collins J. Foster

Emory Clyde Fox
David Nolen Gentry
Dexter Ewing Givens
Governor W. Graham
Cecil Green
Hillard Green
Bennie F. Hargrove
James Harper
Henry Harrison Jr.
Harold Duane Hays
James G. Hicks Jr.
Jimmie S. Hill
James E. Holder
Felix Clark Hood
William Everett Horton
Robert H. Howell Jr.
Arthur Jennette
William S. Jones
Robert G. Kennedy
Delmer King
Carl W. Landwehr
William W. Lynch Jr.
Harry H. McAlister
Earl McCord
James M. Malone
Leo Carlton Martin
Carl Raymond Mayfield
James B. Meeks Jr.
Clarence E. Morrow
Van North
Harry F. Oliphant
Bert Overstrom
John Overton
Vallie Pope
Elmer F. Poteete

W. B. Reese
Shady Ed. Pulley
Roy Lee Ray
Walter Frank Redmon
Herbert B. Reed
Frank M. Reese
John T. Reynolds Jr.
W. A. Robinson
Edward W. Sawyer Jr.
Reedy A. Sears
Cecil Sims Jr.
Walter Kenneth Smith
Elbert H. Spence
Marvin L. Stephens
Clyde Stewart
James Hollis Stinson
Buford Stinson
Edward C. Stolp
Leonard B. Sweeney
Owen T. Sweeney
Roy W. Taylor
Mack Terry Jr.
Leighton C. Varden
George A. Vaughan
William L. Vaughn
Hunter M. Von Hoff
Warren Caldwell Walden
John Rowe Waldren
J. D. Wallace
Bruce L. Widwick
Joe Wilburn
Louie G. Williams Jr.
Ulysses Wray
Herman M. Young Jr.

WILLIAMSON COUNTY, TENNESSEE
Location: Williamson County Library, Franklin

ROLL OF HONOR
KOREAN WAR

1950–1953
Daniel Cartwright, Henry E. Daugherty, Ernest Haynes, George C. Hood, James R. Jamison, Tommy Johnson, Robert A. Lee, James C. Rader, Wiley D. Roseberry

WILLIAMSON COUNTY, TENNESSEE
Location: Williamson County Library entrance, Franklin

ROLL OF HONOR
VIETNAM WAR

1965–1973
Larry G. Buford, Richard L. Carothers, James B. Conway, James A. Cunningham, William M. Goins, Charles H. Hardison, Robert O. Marlin, Danny G. Martin, James E. Peay, John W. Woods Jr.

Location: Williamson County Library entrance, Franklin

West Main Street homes of J. L. Parkes (above) and Reverend A. N. Cunningham (inse

HINCHEYVILLE

In early 1819, Alfred Balch, Felix Grundy, James Irwin, Randal McGavock, and James Trimble developed Hincheyville, Franklin's first subdivision. The ninety acres extending from Fair Street to Eleventh Avenue, included 26 lots on Fair Street, 25 lots on Main Street and 8 lots on Bridge Street. The subdivision was named for Hinchey Petway a wealthy merchant, who had owned the land and whose fine brick home, built across Main Street approximately 90 yards west, had to be razed. Hincheyville was listed on the National Register of Historic Places in 1982.

HERITAGE FOUNDATION
OF FRANKLIN AND WILLIAMSON COUNTY, 1993
Location: West Main Street, Franklin

CITY CEMETERY

The two-acre City Cemetery was deeded by Joel Parrish in 1811 to the town commissioners for $100. Among the early settlers buried here are Ewen Cameron, who built Franklin's first house, and Thomas Stuart, who served as judge of the Fourth Circuit District from its creation in 1809 until 1836. Also in this cemetery are the graves of Col. and Mrs. Guilford Dudley Sr. Colonel Dudley, born in Caroline County, Virginia, in 1756, is one of four Revolutionary War Soldiers buried here. The others are David Squier, Miles Priest, and Moses Priest. The stone gates were erected by the Old Glory Chapters D.A.R. in 1916 "in honor of the pioneer men and women buried here."

ERECTED BY THE FRANKLIN NOON ROTARY CLUB
WILLIAMSON COUNTY HISTORICAL SOCIETY, 1999
Location: Fourth Avenue North, Franklin

City Cemetery, resting place of city pioneers

Dr. D. B. Cliffe

John B. McEwen

REST HAVEN CEMETERY

In 1855, eminent Franklin lawyer John Marshall gave a seven-acre lot for a new cemetery to be located immediately west of the City Cemetery. Early Methodist minister Thomas L. Douglass and numerous Confederate soldiers are buried here. Among the latter is Capt. "Tod" Carter, who was mortally wounded during the Battle of Franklin. Also interred here are post-Civil War Franklin leaders John B. McEwen and Dr. Daniel Cliffe. McEwen was an entrepreneur, lawyer, and owner of Fernvale Springs. Dr. Cliffe was a respected physician, Confederate surgeon, and president of the Nashville and Decatur Railroad. He is buried with family members including his daughter, Belle, and her husband, Gen. James P. Brownlow, U.S.A.

WILLIAMSON COUNTY HISTORICAL SOCIETY, 1996
Location: Fourth Avenue North, Franklin

An 1880 view of Columbia Pike

FEDERAL BREASTWORKS
BATTLE OF FRANKLIN

The breastworks, thirty yards south, were held by Grose's Brigade, Kimball's Division of the Fourth U.S. Army Corps on Nov. 30, 1864. Around 5 P.M., the brigade was attacked by two regiments of Finley's Florida Brigade, C.S.A. The Floridians withdrew and attacked one-half hour later with the entire brigade, but were driven back. Chalmer's Division of Forrest's Cavalry next attacked Kimball's Division from the northwest. A Federal general called this assault, which also was repulsed, "short but severe . . ."

SAVE THE FRANKLIN BATTLEFIELD ASSOCIATION AND
THE FAMILY OF JAMES W. HICKMAN, 1996
Location: Highway 96 West, Franklin

HARD BARGAIN

In 1873, W. S. McLemore subdivided 15 acres, which he called "Hard Bargain" because of a difficult land deal struck in 1866. Hard Bargain became a stable community, largely African-American. The Harvey McLemore house on this lot, built in 1880, was the home of a successful ex-slave and his descendants for 117 years. To the north stands the Franklin Primitive Baptist Church, organized in 1867, and Mt. Hope Cemetery, begun in 1875. On the east stood St. John's Episcopal Church, the church's Negro mission, and a tobacco warehouse. Due south was the 1910 subdivision of Franklin banker E. E. Green and the Green Street Church of God. On the west stood Polk Town, a row of shotgun houses, now a playground.

WILLIAMSON COUNTY HISTORICAL SOCIETY, 1997
Location: Eleventh Avenue North and Glass Street, Franklin

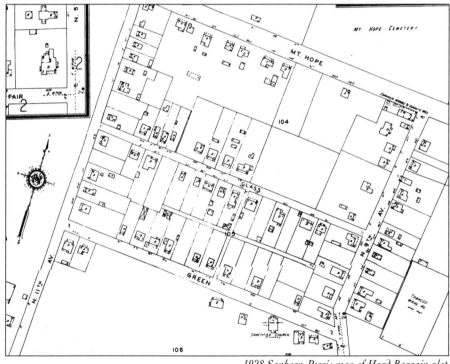

1928 Sanborn-Perris map of Hard Bargain plot

Tombstone in Toussaint L'Ouverture Cemetery of Franklin's oldest merchant

Toussaint L'Ouverture Cemetery

This cemetery is named for Toussaint L'Ouverture, a slave leader whose rebellion led to Haiti's independence in 1804. The cemetery is the final resting place for many Williamson County African-Americans. Among the ex-slaves buried here are A.N.C. Williams, local merchant and minister, and Mariah Otey Reddick, of Carnton Plantation. Grave sites date to 1869 and include veterans of both World Wars, and the Korean and Vietnam conflicts. Many resting here, while nameless, were active citizens of the Baptist Neck, Belltown, and Hard Bargain neighborhoods, offering their labor and domestic skills for the betterment of Franklin. The cemetery was placed on the National Register of Historic Places in 1996.

WILLIAMSON COUNTY HISTORICAL SOCIETY, 1997
Location: Del Rio Pike, Franklin

Matthew Fontaine Maury

MATTHEW FONTAINE MAURY

1.4 miles west stood the home of "The Pathfinder of the Seas." In 1825 he became an officer in the U.S. Navy; after secession, in the Confederate Navy. For discoveries and inventions, he was awarded more decorations by foreign govt. than any American up to that time.

TENNESSEE HISTORICAL COMMISSION
Location: Hillsboro Road, Franklin
Correction: Maury's boyhood home was located near Boyd's Mill six miles west of Franklin.

HARPETH ACADEMY

1.4 miles west, and north of the road, this boys' school commenced operations in 1811 under Rev. Gideon Blackburn, noted Presbyterian missionary. James Hervey Otey, later first Episcopal bishop of Tennessee, succeeded him in 1821. In 1825, the school was moved into Franklin, closing in 1863 when Federal troops destroyed the buildings.

TENNESSEE HISTORICAL COMMISSION
Location: Hillsboro Road, Franklin

Beautiful stone fence enclosing the DeGraffenreid Cemetery

DeGraffenreid Cemetery

Buried here is one of Franklin's first settlers, Metcalfe DeGraffenreid (1760–1803), a Lunenburg County, Virginia native. Three of his sons, Abram, Metcalfe Jr., and Matthew Fontaine, were veterans of the War of 1812. One of them, Metcalfe Jr. is buried here. DeGraffenreid's wife, Mary Ann Maury, sister of Franklin's founder, Abram Maury, is buried in Alabama. Also interred here is one of their three daughters, Susan DeGraffenreid Reese, wife of Beverly Reese; a grandson, Ben DeGraffenreid (1838–1859); a granddaughter, Elizabeth Reese Currin; her husband, John M. Currin; their daughter, Susan; and Katy Ewin (1858–1859), infant daughter of Metcalfe Jr.'s daughter, Catherine, and her second husband, John H. Ewin.

WILLIAMSON COUNTY HISTORICAL SOCIETY, 1999
Location: Glass Lane, north of Highway 96 West, Franklin

MAJOR ANTHONY SHARPE (1746-1812)

 This Revolutionary War veteran of McCroy's Company, Ninth N.C. Regiment, was granted 3,840 acres of land in the new Tennessee county of Williamson. His holdings covered six square miles from Winstead Hill to Roper's Knob. Included were 109 acres on which Abram Maury, who bought 640 acres from Sharpe, laid out the town of Franklin. In 1791, Sharpe married Margaret Nelson of Sumner County, N.C. They had eight children—Sara Sharpe Henry, Jane Sharpe Brodnax, Elizabeth Sharpe Jones, Ann Sharpe McPhail, Sala Sharpe, Searcy Sharpe, Sumner Sharpe, and Margaret Sharpe. After Sharpe's death, his widow married George Hulme (1761–1835), a Revolutionary War veteran and early Williamson County sheriff.

WILLIAMSON COUNTY HISTORICAL SOCIETY, 1999
Location: Boyd's Mill Pike, across from soccer field, Franklin

Grave of Revolutionary War soldier Anthony Sharpe

Abram Maury, Franklin's first developer

ABRAM MAURY

Abram Maury (1866–1825) came to this area from Virginia in 1797 to settle on 640 acres he purchased from Major Anthony Sharpe. In 1798, he reserved a square-shaped area of 109 acres for a town he intended to name Marthaville for his wife. Instead, the town was named Franklin in honor of Benjamin Franklin. Maury, who was a prosperous planter, surveyor and state senator, donated lands for a public square, streets, and a Methodist Church. His log home, Treelawn, stood a short distance north. The nearby family cemetery, where he and Martha are buried, remains inside Founder's Pointe.

WILLIAMSON COUNTY HISTORICAL SOCIETY, 1994
Location: Highway 96 West, Franklin

Fitzgerald School on Coleman Road

AFRICAN-AMERICAN SCHOOLS IN FRANKLIN

From 1888 until 1967 African-American students in Franklin were educated on this site. First known as Claiborne Institute in honor of Prof. Willis Claiborne (1862–1892), later schools here were known as Franklin Colored (1907–1925), Franklin Training (1925–1961), and Natchez High (1961–1967). The present building, known as Claiborne-Hughes Health Center since 1982, was built in 1949. Johnson Elementary School, built in 1958 on Glass Lane, relieved the crowded campus. Principals here were W. F. Reynolds, Maggie Washington, Carrie Otey, James K. Hughes, Dr. I. H. Hampton, E. E. Pitts, J. R. Watkins, and Charles B. Spencer. Integration of public schools was realized in the fall of 1967, 13 years after the Brown vs. Board of Education lawsuit.

HERITAGE FOUNDATION
OF FRANKLIN AND WILLIAMSON COUNTY, 1999
Location: Natchez Street, Franklin

Historical Markers of Williamson County

Students and faculty, Franklin Training School on Natchez Street

AFRICAN-AMERICAN SCHOOLS IN WILLIAMSON COUNTY

Following the Civil War, the Freedmen's Bureau opened schools across Williamson County for the education of the recently emancipated slaves, who had numbered over 12,000 in 1860. With the establishment of a public school system in 1873, Williamson County children attended segregated, mostly one-room-schools. The African-American county schools included Allison, Beechville, Boxley Valley, Boyd, Brentwood, Cedar Hill, Fitzgerald, Florenceville, Green Grove, Goose Creek, Hill's Valley, Hillsboro, Holt-Edmondson, Huntsville, Kirkland, Lee-Buckner, Linwood, Locust Ridge, Mt. LaVergne, Murfree's Fork, Nolensville, Patton, Pearly Hill, Perkins, Rucker's Chapel, Rural Hill, Shady Grove, Thompson's Station, Watson Hill, and Westwood.

WILLIAMSON COUNTY HISTORICAL SOCIETY, 1999
Location: Natchez Street, Franklin

FRANKLIN BATTLEFIELD — A NATIONAL HISTORIC LANDMARK

Under the provision of the
Historic Sites Act of August 21, 1935
this site possesses
exceptional value
in commemorating and illustrating
the history of the United States.

U.S. DEPARTMENT OF INTERIOR
NATIONAL PARK SERVICE, 1961
Location: The Carter House, 1140 Columbia Avenue, Franklin

Map of the Battlefield of Franklin

F. B. Carter (bottom left) and views of the Carter House that include Moscow B. Jr. and Colonel M. B. Carter standing at the fence (bottom right)

CARTER HOUSE

Built 1830 by Fountain Branch Carter, and in use by three generations of his family. Here was command post of Maj. Gen. Jacob D. Cox, Federal field commander of Schofield's delaying action. The hottest fighting took place just east and south; nearby, Capt. Theodoric Carter, CSA, a son of the family, was mortally wounded.

TENNESSEE HISTORICAL SOCIETY
Location: 1140 Columbia Avenue, Franklin

Tod Carter

Captain Theodoric (Tod) Carter c.s.a.

Born at the Carter House March 24, 1840 and educated at Harpeth Academy. He was an attorney-at-law and Master Mason. Tod enlisted in Co. H, 20th Tenn. Infantry May 1, 1862. Appointed Assistant Quarter Master on Oct. 24, 1862 and served as a war correspondent for the Chattanooga "Daily Rebel" using the name "Mint Julep."

Capt. Carter participated in most of the Army of Tenn. battles. He was captured at Chattanooga on May 25, 1863, but escaped from a prison train in Pennsylvania Feb. 1864. He returned to the Army in March 1864 serving in the Atlanta & Tenn. campaigns. Mortally wounded 200 yards southwest of his home on Nov. 30, 1864 in the Battle of Franklin and died at the Carter House Dec. 2, 1864.

"Rest, soldier, rest you are not forgotten, for you did not die in vain."

PLAQUE DONATED BY COMPATRIOT G. DAVID CLARK
THE TOD CARTER CAMP #854
SONS OF CONFEDERATE VETERANS
Location: On the grounds of the Carter House,
1140 Columbia Avenue, Franklin

The cenotaph (above) for Cleburne (inset) was once located on Columbia Avenue

CLEBURNE'S DIVISION
ARMY OF TENNESSEE C.S.A.

This division was commanded by Major General Patrick R. Cleburne, and consisted of Granbury's Texas Brigade, Govan's Arkansas Brigade, and Lowery's Mississippi and Alabama Brigade. They were engaged around the Cotton Gin which stood S.E. of the Carter House. It is said that you could always tell where Cleburne's Division was on the field because their division flag was blue with the full moon and was usually to be found at the heaviest fighting. Cleburne's Division lost 53% casualties including their beloved commander.

PLAQUE DONATED BY MR. AND MRS. EUGENE McNEIL
Location: On the grounds of the Carter House,
1140 Columbia Avenue, Franklin

Albert Lotz (right) and his Columbia Avenue home (above)

THE LOTZ HOUSE

Built by Albert Lotz, naturalized citizen from Germany, on 5 acres purchased from Fountain Branch Carter in 1858. It is shown on the official map of the Franklin Battlefield flanked by a regiment of the Union forces commanded by General Opdyke. The Lotz family of five found refuge with the Carter family in the rock-walled cellar of the Carter House during the Battle of Franklin on Nov. 30, 1864. This building was placed on the National Register of Historic Places on Dec. 12, 1976 and was subsequently renovated for office use by Wayne B. Glasgow Jr., in 1983.

WILLIAMSON COUNTY HISTORICAL SOCIETY, 1985
Location: Columbia Avenue, Franklin

An 1880 view of the battle line

Main Entrenchment
Federal Battle Line

Battle of Franklin, November 30, 1864. Federal Commander, Gen. John M. Schofield. Confederate Commander, Gen. John B. Hood. Bloodiest Battle of the war between the States for numbers involved. In this battle fell six Confederate Generals; Cleburne, Strahl, Gist, Adams, Granbury and Carter.

TENNESSEE HISTORICAL COMMISSION, 1922
RESTORED BY S. S. ORWIG, 1936
Location: Columbia Avenue, Franklin

Painting of the Carter Gin House after the battle

CARTER GIN HOUSE

The Carter cotton gin house, the scene of some of the bloodiest fighting of the Battle of Franklin, was located about 80 yards east of Columbia Pike. Generals Adams, Cleburne, and Granbury were killed near here. The gin house, a weatherboarded, frame structure, was 36 feet square with massive 24" X 36" poplar sills to carry the weight of the heavy gin machinery. The sills rested on 8-foot-high stone pillars thus providing head room for horses which powered the gin by walking in a circle pulling a boom pole. The Federals stripped the structure for materials to be used in the breastworks. About 20 yards in front of the gin were breastworks with deep outer ditches.

The Carter gin house marked a projection in the breastworks. A short distance west of the gin, the works made an angle toward the rear. On this ground Cleburne, French, and a portion of Brown and Walthall's Confederate Divisions engaged Reilly and Casement's Federal Brigades. Maj. Gen. Patrick Cleburne was killed 40 to 50 yards south of the gin. Brig. Gen. H. B. Granbury was killed on the turnpike 80 yards from the works. Brig. Gen. John Adams, mortally wounded, was carried by the Federals to the gin, where they placed cotton beneath his head. Brig. Gen. George W. Gordon was wounded and captured near the angle of the works. The Confederate dead of these divisions were buried in the outer ditch.

SAVE THE FRANKLIN BATTLEFIELD, INC.
WILLIAMSON COUNTY HISTORICAL SOCIETY, 1998
Location: Cleburne Street, east of Columbia Avenue, Franklin

Scenes of BGA, including BGA's oldest buildings on the postcard (top)

BATTLE GROUND ACADEMY

Founded in 1889 as Battle Ground Academy, named for its location where the Battle of Franklin occurred in 1864, and dedicated in an address by Confederate General William B. Bate, later governor and U.S. Senator, this boys' preparatory school was located on Columbia Avenue across from the Carter House. The school was popularly called the Wall and Mooney School and the Peoples School for its early headmasters. After being destroyed by fire in 1902, it was moved to its present site.

TENNESSEE HISTORICAL COMMISSION
Location: Columbia Avenue, Franklin

Winstead Hill's view of the battlefield

BATTLE OF FRANKLIN

Here occurred one of the most desperately fought battles of the entire War Between the States. Between Union forces of Gen. John M. Schofield and the attacking Confederate Army of Tennessee under Gen. John B. Hood.

Maj. Gen. George H. Thomas commanding Union Tennessee Dept. had placed forces of Schofield in the area around Pulaski, Tenn. 50 miles south to contest Hood's advance north into Tennessee. Hood's intent was to move to Nashville, there to Union forces under Thomas, thus cutting rail and other supply lines to Sherman and other Union forces in Atlanta-Chattanooga areas. As Hood drove northward Schofield retreated, until overtaken by Hood at Columbia (23 miles south).

Crossing the Duck River at Columbia, Hood almost succeeded in getting in Schofield's rear at Spring Hill (10 miles south), but due to a miscarriage of Confederate orders Schofield escaped northward when within gunshot of the Confederate forces.

Enraged and frustrated Hood threw most of his army, but with very little artillery present, against the strongest part of Schofield's forces.

The Battle Of Franklin
November 30th, 1864

Editor's Note: As the reader is probably aware, Mr. Will McGann is known state wide for the beauty and distinctiveness of his many poems. His more recent contribution is published bellow:

By WILL S. McGANN

Low in the west the autumn sun poised in a darkening sky,
As the thin gray lines went proudly on, to victory—or to die,
Their tattered flags had waived above a hundred desperate fights,
And now they flapped in the evening breeze from the tree-clad Harpeth heights.

Shoulder to shoulder, on they went to where death crouched to slay,
The fate of a nation marched with them, those dauntless men in gray,
The fate of a nation rested there on the points of their bayonets bright,
And never a man but pledged his all to the Cause that he knew was Right.

The fields were furrowed with rifle pits that blossomed in flame and smoke,
But the fearless gray lines onward came, and the blue-clad enemy broke;
Broke and scattered like frightened quail at the terrible yell,
And the men in gray swept on that day to the open mouth of hell.

Into the yawning jaws of hell, scorched by its fiery breath
Over the yankee works they poured, those men who laughed at death.
Over the trench that streamed with blood, and the mound of crimsoned

To win from the foe that crouched below the soil that gave them birth.

Death was busy, that dreadful eve, with a scythe of fire and lead,
With the morning sun, when the fight was done, the flower of the South lay dead.

Dead on the field they would not yield, those heroes in faded gray,
And bright on the roll of valor's scroll is the fame they won that day.

Under the sod and the dew they rest in dreamless slumber deep,
While the years drift past till the Trumpet blast shall rouse them from their sleep;

Then up from the earth that gave them birth, up from their blood-bought sod,
...e Men in Gray shall stand that day at the great right hand of God.

Battlefield scenes (left) and a poem by
Will S. McGann (above)

About 16,000 Confederates were in the action, the Corps of Stephen D. Lee and most of the artillery having been left at Columbia to detain Schofield.

The attack was brief but bloody: the Confederates made furious charges between 3:30 and 9:00 P.M. with severe losses. In two Confederate brigades, all general and field officers were killed or wounded; a major commanded Brown's entire division at the end of the action.

In two Confederate assaulting corps, a major general, five brigadier and 13 regimental commanders were killed; a major general, 4 brigadiers and 33 regimental commanders wounded, with one brigadier general captured, 8 regimental commanders were missing. Total Confederate casualties were over 6,300 in killed, wounded and missing. Union forces numbered about 22,000 most of whom were in action. Killed, wounded and missing number over 2,300. One general officer was wounded.

By midnight, November 30, Schofield withdrew to Nashville: Hood followed closely the next day and invested the city. The decisive Battle of Nashville followed Dec. 15–16.

Location: Overlook at Winstead Hill, U.S. Highway 31, Franklin

General John Bell Hood, C.S.A.   *Major General John M. Schofield*

HOOD AND SCHOFIELD

Nov. 30, 1864. Schofield, slipping his army past Hood's at Spring Hill, entrenched in the southern edge of Franklin, 2 mi. N. Here Hood attacked him, frontally about 4 P.M., sustaining heavy losses. Schofield withdrew to Nashville. Hood followed. Hood's command post during the battle was on top of the slope 50 yds. west.

TENNESSEE HISTORICAL COMMISSION
Location: Overlook at Winstead Hill, U.S. Highway 31, Franklin

THE HARRISON HOUSE

The Civil War touched this house. Here, Sept. 2, 1964, the mortally wounded Brig. Gen. John H. Kelley, CSA, was brought after the affair between his cavalry division and the Federals under Brig. Gen. James D. Brownlow. He was buried in the garden, in 1868 reinterred in Mobile. Here Gen. Hood held his last staff conference before committing his army to the Battle of Franklin Nov. 30, 1864. Here the wounded Brig. Gen. John C. Carter was brought after the battle. He died Dec. 10, 1864, and was buried in Columbia, 16 mi. south.

TENNESSEE HISTORICAL SOCIETY
Location: U.S. Highway 31, south of Franklin

The Harrison House, home of William Harrison, antebellum sheriff

An 1880 view of Henry Fowlkes's and James McNutt's homes on Lewisburg Avenue

LEWISBURG AVENUE
HISTORIC DISTRICT

This Historic District, located along Lewisburg Ave. immediately south of what once was the town limit, consisted of 31 houses in 1993. The district's oldest residence is the Otey-Campbell House, built in 1840 on the corner of South Margin and Lewisburg Ave. In a house across the street, long since torn down, Mrs. Canelm Hines ran the Franklin Grove Girls' School from 1829 until her death in the 1850s. Later, her son-in-law, James A. McNutt, was principal of Carnton High School, which was located in the same building.

The well-preserved and maintained residences in the district display a variety of styles, including Queen Anne, Italianate, Colonial Revival, Bungalow, and English Tudor.

HERITAGE FOUNDATION
OF FRANKLIN AND WILLIAMSON COUNTY
WILLIAMSON COUNTY HISTORICAL SOCIETY, 1993
Location: Lewisburg Avenue and South Margin Street, Franklin

Historical Markers of Williamson County

Willow Plunge, Franklin's summer playground

WILLOW PLUNGE

Opened in 1924, this was the largest outdoor concrete swimming pool in the South. Willow Plunge was owned, and for many years operated, by the Claiborne Kinnard family. Water was piped 1,023 feet from a spring to the willow-shaded double pool which measured 75 X 150 feet and had a capacity of 750,000 gallons. The water was treated by the latest scientific methods of purification and was pure enough to be used for drinking. In 1932 Willow Plunge was named one of the six best equipped pools in the United States. Additional features included a tennis court, 9–hole golf course, miniature golf course, football field, aviation field, and lake. Willow Plunge closed in 1965.

WILLIAMSON COUNTY HISTORICAL SOCIETY, 1999
Location: Carnton Lane and Lewisburg Pike, Franklin

Confederate Cemetery

CONFEDERATE CEMETERY

Following the Battle of Franklin, Nov. 30, 1864, John McGavock collected and buried here the bodies of 1,496 Confederates. Other Confederates were later buried here, including Brig. Gen. Johnston K. Duncan.

TENNESSEE HISTORICAL COMMISSION
Location: Carnton Lane, Franklin

Historical Markers of Williamson County

McGavock
Confederate Cemetery

In the spring of 1866, Col. John McGavock, seeing the deteriorating condition of the Confederate graves on the Franklin battlefield, set aside two acres of Carnton Plantation as the nation's largest private Confederate cemetery. The dead were reinterred here in order by states. In 1890, the wooden markers, which were inscribed with the names of the men, their companies and regiments, when known, were replaced with stone markers. Burial records were preserved by Col. McGavock's wife, the former Carrie Winder. She and her husband maintained the cemetery for the balance of their lives.

WILLIAMSON COUNTY HISTORICAL SOCIETY, 1994
Location: Confederate Cemetery at Carnton, Franklin

McGavock Confederate Cemetery, Franklin, honors the fallen sons of the Lost Cause

Carrie Winder McGavock   *Colonel John McGavock*

McGavock Family Cemetery

Buried here, beginning ca. 1818, are the remains of numerous family members. Among them are Randal McGavock (1768–1843), planter and political leader who built Carnton; his son, Col. John McGavock (1815–1843), successful farmer and civic leader who was instrumental in disinterring the Confederate dead from the Franklin battlefield and reburying them adjacent to this cemetery; and John's wife, Carrie Winder McGavock (1829–1905). This venerable Southern mother was called "The Good Samaritan of Williamson County" for her many acts of loving service to Confederate soldiers.

WILLIAMSON COUNTY HISTORICAL SOCIETY, 1994
Location: McGavock Cemetery at Carnton, Franklin

CARNTON PLANTATION

Carnton was built ca. 1815 by Randal McGavock (1768–1843), planter, political leader and mayor of Nashville. Named after the McGavock home in Northern Ireland, the house was greatly enlarged by Randal ca. 1826. His son, John, later added the Greek Revival porches, one of which served as an observation post for Gen. Nathan B. Forrest during the Battle of Franklin, Nov. 30, 1864. After the Battle, Carnton served as a hospital. The bodies of General Adams, Cleburne, Granbury, and Strahl rested on the back porch by the Carnton Association in 1979.

WILLIAMSON COUNTY HISTORICAL SOCIETY, 1994
Location: Carnton Lane, Franklin

Carnton with cedar- and boxwood-lined brick entrance

Premier Delight, the first Tennessee Walking Horse to be shown in Europe, with J. W. Cross III, owner

PREMIER DELIGHT
No. 733592

January 4, 1973 — November 6, 1984
1977
Junior World Champion
1980
Ambassador to England
"He carried the Banner Proudly"
Tuck-Away Farms
Mr. and Mrs. J. Wm. Cross III
Franklin, Tennessee
Pride's Mr. Showman 1974–1981
Pride's Big Storm 1977–1984
Summer Fest 1977–1984

Location: Tuck-Away Farm, 1190 Lewisburg Pike, Franklin

EDWARD CURD SR.

On a hill a short distance N.W. of the Williamson Medical Center stands the home of Edward Curd Sr., son of Price and Elizabeth Hall Curd of Wilson County, Tenn. The farm was formerly known as the Thomas J. Carothers place. Born in Wilson County, Mr. Curd (1845–1916) served in Freeman's Battery of Light Artillery, C.S.A. In 1867, he married Josephine Owen (1846–1919) and with his family moved to Williamson County in 1881. The Curd apple orchards stretched from his home southward toward Murfreesboro Pike.

WILLIAMSON MEDICAL CENTER
WILLIAMSON COUNTY HISTORICAL SOCIETY, 1988
Location: Edward Curd Lane at Highway 96, Franklin
Correction: The Carothers-Curd House was moved to West Main, Franklin

Edward Curd Sr.

McConnico Meeting House (above in 1909), a Primitive Baptist church organized by Reverend Garner McConnico (inset)

McConnico Meeting House

About 100 yards SW stood the church where Garner McConnico, a pioneer from Lunenburg County, Va., organized a Primitive Baptist congregation about 1799. Destroyed by storm in 1909, the church was rebuilt at its present location on the Liberty Pike, about 3 miles NW. The old cemetery remains.

TENNESSEE HISTORICAL SOCIETY
Location: Highway 96 East near Clovercroft Road, Franklin
Additional Information: The present congregation is called Big Harpeth Primitive Baptist Church.

INDEX

Marker names are indicated by bold entries. Numbers in bold indicate a photograph or illustration.

Historical Markers of Williamson County